99

Ninetynine

NICK NAMED

Classic Cars

HELGE JEPSEN / ILLUSTRATIONS
MICHAEL KÖCKRITZ / TEXTS

a**ramp**book

teNeues

Nicknames for cars? An ingenious idea! Flirty, alluring, quirky, or downright disrespectful—in general, it is the unique cars with timeless designs and enthralling anecdotes that pique one's interest for the pastime of name-finding. Hence our inspiration for this project.

Our original idea was for a niche article for the cars and culture magazine, *ramp*. With lady luck on our side, we banked on identifying perhaps twelve to fifteen nicknamed cars, with evocative illustrations and accompanying texts to captivate the reader with a hall of renowned nicknames. That was then. Now, we realize the need for more space. A lot more space. Serious amounts of space—not only magazine pages.

Finally, our brainwave for an eye-catching series in a car magazine morphed into this book—the likelihood is that it will claim the title as the standard work of classic-automobiles-with-nicknames world literature. Nonetheless, the pleasure was entirely ours in devising its concept and nurturing its development.

And now for the important part—it's time for this book to beguile its owner with inspirational stories about car nomenclature.

In this spirit: Enjoy the drive!

PS: Of course, we take our research seriously and we have paid meticulous attention to detail. Inevitably, however, a savvy car lover will most likely suggest a previously unknown fact. Be our guest! We welcome all your annotations and corrections. No later than the 32nd edition, we will certainly take these on board. That's a promise.

Helge Jepsen, illustrations / Michael Köckritz, texts

AAR EAGLE T1G

"SHARK"

California-based Dan Gurney made his Formula 1 career with the official All American Racers team, or AAR. The Eagle T1G single-seater turned heads with its aggressive front end. Many trackside fans found it reminiscent of a shark's snout, so Gurney's car was nicknamed "Shark." In 1966, Gurney still raced a 2.75-liter four-cylinder Coventry Climax engine. That engine was seriously under-powered and already outdated. The AAR "Shark's" competitive streak only came to light when the 420 hp, 3.0-liter Weslake V12 was built. Several technical glitches had to be mastered. With its first and only victory at the Belgian GP at Spa-Francorchamps, Gurney's T1G finished ahead of Britain's Jackie Stewart, driving for B.R.M., and New Zealander Chris Amon's third in a Ferrari. To add to his race legend reputation, in 1971, Dan Gurney lent his All-American driver ID to the Gurney Flap—a small, vertical, right-angle flap on the rear wing. This aerodynamic innovation creates more downforce over the rear axle without jeopardizing air resistance. Today, it is still standard on all racing cars. Another popular invention: Dan Gurney was the first driver to fizz up a champagne shower after a win.

1966	2.750-2.996 CC	260-423 HP	N/A

ALFA ROMEO 40-60 HP AERODINAMICA

"SILURO RICOTTI"

Despite its weird appearance, this Alfa was revered as top of the line. It was the company's biggest model in 1914, its launch year. "Siluro" meaning "torpedo" epitomizes its shape and speed—topping out at 85 mph (139 km/h), this vehicle had a season ticket for the inside lane. Or it would have had, if the autostrada network had existed then. Marco Ricotti commissioned the car from Carrozzeria Castagna. But he'd soon had enough of its restricted view, noise, and heat in the cabin. In a few months, he had decided to turn it into an open tourer. A replica of the limousine is now housed in the Museo Storico Alfa Romeo in Arese. Strictly speaking, the car's name should be written A.L.F.A. 40-60 HP, after the company's official name till November 23, 1919, standing for Societa Anonima Lombarda Fabbrica Automobili, or simply the Lombardy Car Factory Company. Alfa Romeo became the firm's official brand name much later.

1914	6.082 CC	73 HP	85 MPH

ALFA ROMEO 1900 C52

"FLYING SAUCER"

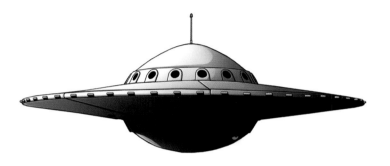

This Alfa is, and henceforth shall be, one of the most intriguing classic models. But it was probably best for a smaller-than-average driver as one felt perpetual claustrophobia, like sitting in a child's car with scaled-down proportions. The legendary bodywork was created by coachbuilding firm Touring. Its performance was outstanding, even by today's standards: 158 hp at 6,500 rpm and weighing in at just 1620 lbs (735 kg). The coupé was built on the Spider variant; its body design also necessitated employing a simulator model in a wind tunnel to keep things under wraps as Alfa Romeo's C52 originally targeted motorsport. An entire team was put together for the 1953 Mille Miglia, equipped with four coupés. One car was running a four-cylinder engine, while the other three had six-cylinder alternatives. It was no recipe for success, even with Juan Manuel Fangio behind the wheel—he was outrun by a Ferrari just before the finish. Equally unsuccessful at Le Mans, the car's only win to date is a modest victory in the Grand Prix Supercortemaggiore. But to keep it with Henry Ford, who supposedly lauded its timeless design: "When I see an Alfa, I always raise my hat."

1953	1.997 CC	158 HP	140 MPH

ALFA ROMEO SPIDER

"OSSO DI SEPPIA"

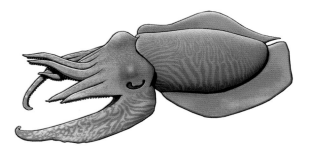

Beautiful mothers have beautiful daughters. So said Dustin Hoffman as Benjamin Braddock in *The Graduate*, as he cruised in his red Alfa Romeo past American limos toward his tryst with Anne Bancroft, *aka* Mrs. Robinson. Hoffman rose to stardom with the 1967 movie and in doing so, secured worldwide fame for the Alfa Romeo Spider. Public opinion was split when the little Alfa was launched in 1966. Production line workers gave it the nickname "Osso di Seppia,"—the internal bone of the cuttlefish—to highlight its rear shape. A write-in competition was held for a new name with first prize being a pristine car straight off the production line. The public submitted 120,000 catchy ideas like "Pizza", "Sputnik" or "Lollobrigida". The winner was "Duetto", although it was replaced with the launch of the 1750 Veloce. "Duetto" still captured the public imagination and was used for all round-tailed Spider models, although that's far from being politically correct. But then neither was Benjamin Braddock's affair with Mrs. Robinson.

1966-1969	1.570 CC	109 HP	115 MPH

AMC PACER

"FLYING FISHBOWL"

Size is relative. Compared with a BMW Isetta an AMC Pacer seems like the mothership. But compared with a Dodge Ram this automobile must fight to be taken seriously as a proper car. That said, even a full-grown SUV would hardly make an impact. With its 6-ft (2-m) girth, the AMC Pacer is a princely size by European standards, even if this vehicle presents contradictions: big on the outside but with space for only two people and their luggage on the inside, daringly modern, yet somehow dated. Its design was revolutionary in its day. Thirty-seven percent of its surface was glass, creating an impressive all-round view but also earning it the enduring nickname "Flying Fishbowl." The Pacer also introduced new innovations in production; it was the first mass-produced U.S. car based on the cab-forward concept, i.e., the driver's position moved further forward than in traditionally manufactured cars. Trade magazines described the AMC Pacer as the 1970s answer to future automotive visions of the U.S. cartoon series "The Jetsons."

1975-1980	4.229 CC	110 HP	100 MPH

ASTON MARTIN DB5

"BOND CAR"

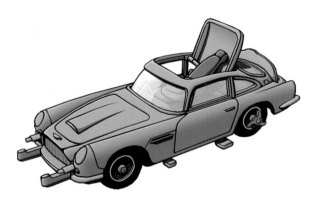

Bond actors may come and go, but the Aston Martin DB5 is here to stay. The archetypal Bond car made its debut in the mid-1960s in *Goldfinger* and *Thunderball*. A four-liter, six-cylinder engine gave the secret agent a sweet drive with 286 hp. Additional features such as a machine gun, ejector seat or removable shield for the rear window were exclusive luxuries for the secret service. Although Ian Fleming sent Bond on missions in a DB Mark III, the film producers opted for the current DB model at the time, using a prototype with chassis number 1486. The iconographic DB5 has since featured in the latest Bond movies such as *Goldeneye, Tomorrow Never Dies, Casino Royale, Skyfall,* and *Spectre*. While the DB5 usually starred in a cameo role, it again played lead as getaway car in *Skyfall*, testing out its weaponry anew. By the end of the movie, the bad guys had almost totaled the DB5, but Q restored it so the final scenes of *Spectre* show Bond driving away in the car. He needed it—by then, he'd already sunk his DB10 in the Tiber in Rome.

1963-1965	3.995 CC	286 HP	140 MPH

AUDI SPORT QUATTRO E2

"PIKES PEAK"

After scoring multiple victories in Audi Quattro variants from 1982, the Ingolstadt factory revealed the short version Sport Quattro in 1984. Stig Blomqvist raced it to an opening victory in the Rallye Côte d'Ivoire. In its debut 1985 full season, the short wheelbase Quattro was at a technical disadvantage compared with its mid-engined rivals. After a Ford driver's serious accident at the 1986 Rally Portugal, Audi withdrew from the world rally championship. The Sport Quattro's final developmental phase, the E2, was used for the legendary Pikes Peak International Hill Climb in the U.S. state of Colorado. Audi had no doubts about the prestige of this race—partly run on tarmac and partly on gravel. Starting out at an altitude of 9,390 ft (2,862 m), the finish line is at 14,110 ft (4,301 m). For the 12-mile (20-km) "Race to the Clouds," the five-cylinder turbocharged engine was souped up from 530 to 600 hp, and no lesser driver than Walter Röhrl strapped himself into the sparse cockpit of the savage racing machine. The tall Bavarian was the first to record a time of under eleven minutes: The clock stopped at exactly 10:47 minutes. That win was the ultimate outing for the supreme all-wheel-drive car, since known by its nickname "Pikes Peak." The meteoric short wheelbase Quattro E2 could also manage 0 to 60 mph (0-100 km/h) in just 2.9 seconds. Glorious insanity with attitude.

1987	2.140 CC	600 HP	195 MPH

AUSTIN-HEALEY 3000

"THE PIG"

The Austin Healey 3000—along with Jaguar and Triumph models—was one of the British racing highlights of the 1960s. It rose to fame after Pat Moss, younger sister of racing legend Stirling Moss and Swedish rally star Erik Carlsson's wife, dramatically referred to the two-seater as "The Pig." Moss drove a works Healey and she disliked the rear-engined car's unpredictability that would often throw out its tail without warning. But the British female racing champion (born 1934, died 2008) could clearly handle the Austin's idiosyncrasies, finishing in fourth place in the 1960 Liège-Rome-Liège Rally. By the end of the season, Pat Moss even won the European Ladies' Rally Championship. The Austin Healey was predestined for a career in motorsport: its ultralight construction and torquey 3.0-liter straight-six engine provided superb performance, although its touchy oversteer habit frustrated many racing pros, as well as private owners, ruining the roadster's reputation. Not to mention decimating the number of vehicles on the road.

1959-1967	2.912 CC	124-148 HP	110-120 MPH

AUSTIN-HEALEY SPRITE MKI

"FROGEYE"

Would these (frog) eyes lie to you? No, sir. There were no flies on the Austin Healey Sprite Mk I. This unpretentious little number gave minimal comfort, while promising utmost driving bliss and joyous fresh air. See it, and you instantly think, "This car spells fun—the clue is in the name 'Sprite'." The idea that die-hard enthusiasts named this English roadster after an amphibian ('frogeye') could lull you into a sense of the driver's threshold for discomfort. Firstly, take the higher probability of rain in the British Isles compared with the Continent. Secondly, remember its scant convertible design that now hints at the damp passengers inside. Would frogs feel more at home in the "Frogeye's" soggy ecosystem? Pure speculation. No matter how fun the design seems, with its two unmistakable headlamp bulges on top of the hood, it wasn't a big hit at the time. Countless conversion kits were available for the Frogeye, which led Austin to make some design tweaks: 1961 saw the headlamps migrate outward to the extended, straightened front wings. The Mk II Sprite was in production until 1971, and in terms of numbers, far exceeded the Mk I, made from 1958 to 1961, possibly because the goblin-look with frog's eyes had long gone.

1958-1961	948 CC	42,5 HP	80 MPH

B.R.M. P83

"BRITISH RACING MISERY"

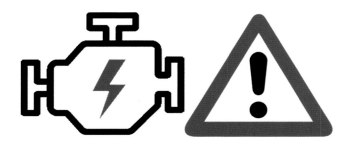

Design ingenuity versus established favorites: In the Formula 1 World Championship, these diverse engine designs once went head to head. This was the engine designers' perfect battle field. Very different from today, where the rule mandates a 1.6-liter V6 turbo engine for all teams. 1960s power plants were limited to around three liters—four-cylinder engines battled against V8s and V12s. The twelve-cylinder engine had yet to reach its peak. British Racing Motors, or B.R.M. for short, used a 16-cylinder racing engine: The H-16. Two eight-cylinder blocks were angled at 180 degrees. Although the H-16 developed 420 hp, its heavy weight made the B.R.M. single-seater extremely tail happy. Also hampered by technical issues, the H-16 never won against conventional V8 and V12 racing cars. Creative motorsport fans wittily christened it "British Racing Misery." The best result this exotic British entrant achieved was second place in the 1967 Belgian Grand Prix, when Jackie Stewart landed the podium place behind the AAR Eagle Shark, driven by Dan Gurney. At the end of the season, the 16-cylinder was retired.

1966-1967	3.000 CC	420 HP	N/A

BENTLEY MARK VI

"THE SILENT SPORTS CAR"

It goes without saying: The Mk VI was made for the upper classes. Incidentally, it was the first post-war model from Bentley Motors and technically based on the Rolls Royce Silver Wraith of the same year, though with a shorter wheelbase and modified engine beneath a new factory body ("Standard Steel"). Initially, the vehicle was fitted with a straight-six engine known as the "4 ¼-liter," and later with a bored out "4 ½-liter" engine—models in turn labelled the small bore and big bore. From day one, the car was unveiled as the "Silent Sports Car" right down to this exclusively entitled manual featuring 23 pages of chassis diagrams and technical data. This hard-to-come-by booklet is highly prized by modern collectors. On rare occasions when one comes up for auction, bidding runs to hundreds of pounds sterling for the book alone.

1946-1952	4.256 CC	N/A	95 MPH

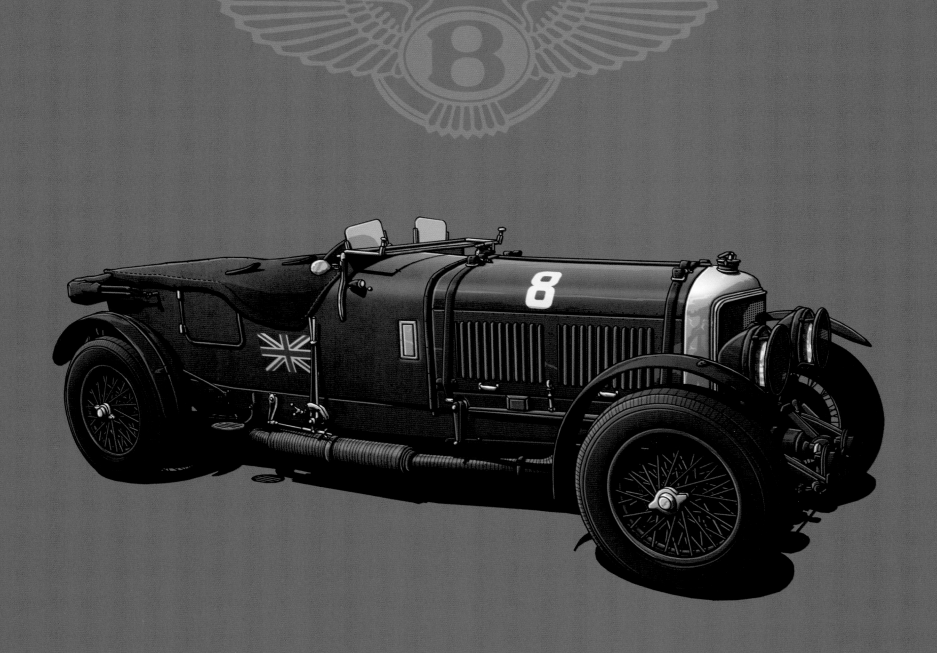

BENTLEY SPEED SIX

"WORLD'S FASTEST TRUCK"

Until 1926, Bentley used 3-liter six-cylinder engines. Affluent clients demanded larger and larger bodies, so the British manufacturer was forced to design a more powerful engine. The 3.0 liters evolved into a new 6.5-liter engine. The massive straight six was a surprise with an extremely modern design for its time: Key features were an overhead camshaft, four valves per cylinder, and dual ignition, making it miles ahead in technical terms. It developed an impressive 180 hp. The sports version with higher compression and twin SU carburetors was designated as the "Speed Six", producing an extra 20 hp. Bentley won the prestigious Le Mans endurance race twice with the "Speed Six": In 1929, the Bentley Boys—Sir Henry Ralph Stanley "Tim" Birkin and Bentley owner Woolf Barnato—were immortalized in the winners' list with the Bentley known as "Old Number One." Three more Bentleys romped home making that four wins. The Brits were destined for massive publicity. One year later, the 24 Hours race was once again headed by a "Speed Six", commonly known as the "World's Fastest Truck" due to its imposing size.

1926-1930	6.597 CC	200 HP	100 MPH

BISCÚTER 100

"CLOG"

A Spanish car maker? Biscúter ticked that box in the early 1950s. Rolling off the production line in Barcelona was its Model 100. Originally, the minimal car design featured no doors, windows or reverse gear; it weighed just 441 lbs (200 kg) and was intended as a commercial vehicle. The Biscúter eventually gained more car-like attributes, and at some point, it even acquired the ability to go backwards. The vehicle was soon given the nickname "Zapatilla," clog or little shoe, after its shape and the common phrase "as ugly as a Biscúter." In 1950, the Spanish government approved a Spanish subsidiary of Italian manufacturer Fiat, going by the name of SEAT, to make cars that were mostly unaffordable for the Spanish population, so the Biscúter still hung around in 1960 when almost 12,000 variants were on the road. Today, an estimated 250 Biscúters remain in existence. The vehicle is a virtual unknown among collectors outside Spain, although there are a few in foreign museums.

1953-1960	197 CC	9,5 HP	50 MPH

BMW 320 GROUP 5

"FLYING BRICK"

What an astonishing transformation! From the narrow, production BMW E21, the motorsport division created a wild, winged monster back in 1977. With a square nose, a shovel-like front spoiler and enormous rear spoiler, the angular tourer made a huge impression. It was an incredible opportunity for fans, who named the BMW 320 the "Flying Brick." Rules from the German Racing Championship for Group 5 cars then allowed this kind of excess; rivals from Ford and Lancia sported a similar hell-raising appearance in the small division. The BMW 320 also became well known through the BMW Junior Team, newly founded by racing director Jochen Neerpasch: Drivers Manfred Winkelhock, Eddie Cheever, and Marc Surer entertained spectators with wild duels against Ford drivers Armin Hahne and Hans Heyer. Scuffed paintwork and dented panels were the order of the day in these hard-fought races. Surer even lost his racing license after a tough battle with Heyer at the Norisring. The fire power beneath the hood was initially provided by the two-liter, normally aspirated four-cylinder engine borrowed from Formula 2, producing 300 hp. The 320 began to flex its muscles later in its life: a 1.4-liter, four-cylinder turbo engine developing 480 hp fired up the BMW to speeds of 180 mph (290 km/h). In 1978, Harald Ertl claimed the championship in this race car.

1977-1982	1.431-1.999 CC	300-480 HP	155-180 MPH

BMW 635 CSI GROUP 2

"SHARK"

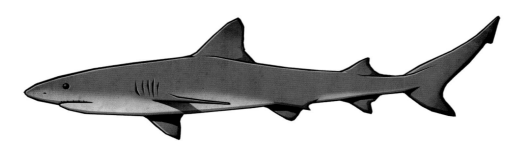

The 635 CSi was the racing circuit heir to the successful 3.0 CSL, so it had some pretty big boots to fill. Like the closely related 5 Series, the Coupé now followed the new nomenclature too. The 6 Series unveiled in 1975, showed BMW styling at its best: its aggressive front end with a pointed kidney grille and downward slanted radiator grille were typical. The twin headlamps were slightly set back beneath the overhanging hood. The Bavarians slavishly perfected this style over many years. Over-taking presence comes as standard. Visually, it evokes a shark's profile. The BMW 635 CSi joined the line-up in 1981 for different race teams, among them, Schnitzer Motorsport's works team. A shortfall of horsepower compared with the Jaguar XJS and Volvo 240 Turbo is a minor distraction because the BMW claimed the hat-trick in the European Touring Car Championship: in 1981, with Helmut Kelleners, Dieter Quester in 1983, and Roberto Ravaglia in 1986. It landed its first German Touring Car Championship/DTM title in 1984, with Volker Strycek at the wheel and the shark-nosed coupé was five-times a winner in the 24-hour races at Spa-Francorchamps and the Nürburgring. The 6 Series caused a sensation on the road too, especially the M 635 CSi. This top-of-the-line model had the four-valve engine under the hood, made famous by the M1 supersports car, developing 286 hp—a genuine Porsche-frightener.

1981-1986	3.430 CC	325 HP	180 MPH

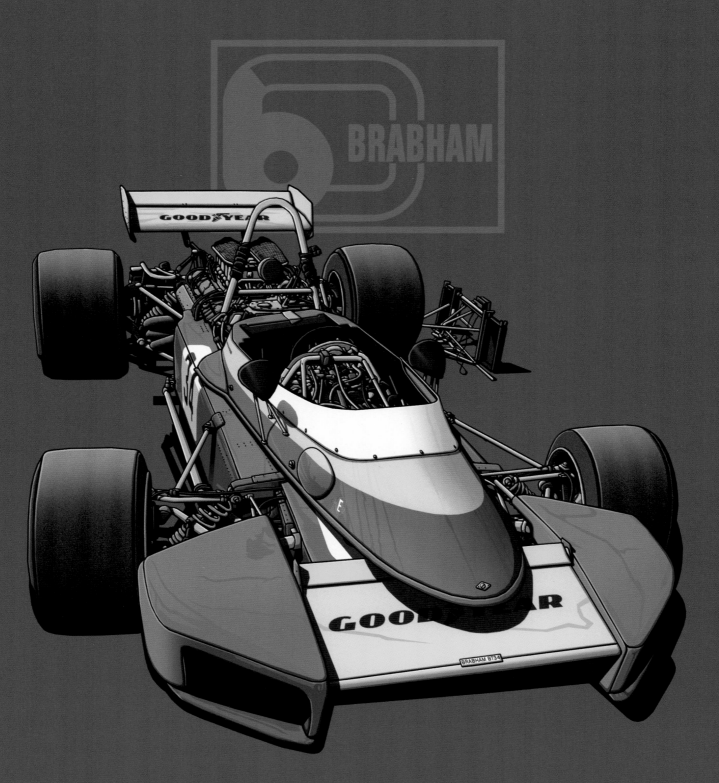

BRABHAM BT34

"LOBSTER CLAW"

The animal kingdom was always a top favorite for nicknames for cars of all types and each era. The Brabham BT34, aka "Lobster Claw" is no exception. Designed by team owner Ron Tauranac, this distinctive front wing was intended—as often occurs in Formula 1—to make the car faster, or at least to improve engine cooling. Two radiators mounted in boxes ahead of the front spoiler controlled temperature regulation. Rectangular air intakes draw the eye almost magically, while the stylishly contrasting green and yellow paintwork does the rest. Beauty lies in the eye of the beholder. (At least, Formula 1 cars of this era had special flair unlike today's repetitive style vehicles.) The Brabham BT34 lined up for the 1971 Formula 1 season alongside the March 711. Neither car won a single race. The legendary British racing driver Graham Hill crossed the line first in his last BRDC Trophy race at Silverstone. Ron Tauranac, who took over the race team from founder Jack Brabham in 1969, sold the Brabham Team in late 1971, to one Bernie Ecclestone.

1971	2.993 CC	400 HP	N/A

BRABHAM BT44

"WHITE BEAUTY"

Minimalist lines, white bodywork, and eye-catching Martini stripes epitomized design allure in 1974. The Brabham BT44's designer was Britain's Gordon Murray. The car was dubbed "White Beauty" by fans. As well as its distinctive tricolor stripes, a Martini logo defined the single-seater's monstrous breather supplying air to the Cosworth DFV V8 engine. With slightly under 3-liter capacity, the engine developed 400 hp at 9,000 rpm. For the 1974 season, the Brabham BT44 team comprised Argentina's Carlos Reutemann, with Carlos Pace, and John Watson. After twice landing seventh in the season's opening races, Reutemann scored his first win at the South African Grand Prix at Kyalami. The Brabham BT44 enjoyed further victories at Zeltweg in Austria and at the Watkins Glen season finale in the United States. Reutemann and Pace each gained one win during the next year. A handful of superb finishes left the Brabham team's "White Beauty" second in the World Constructors' Championship.

1974-1975	2.993 CC	416 HP	N/A

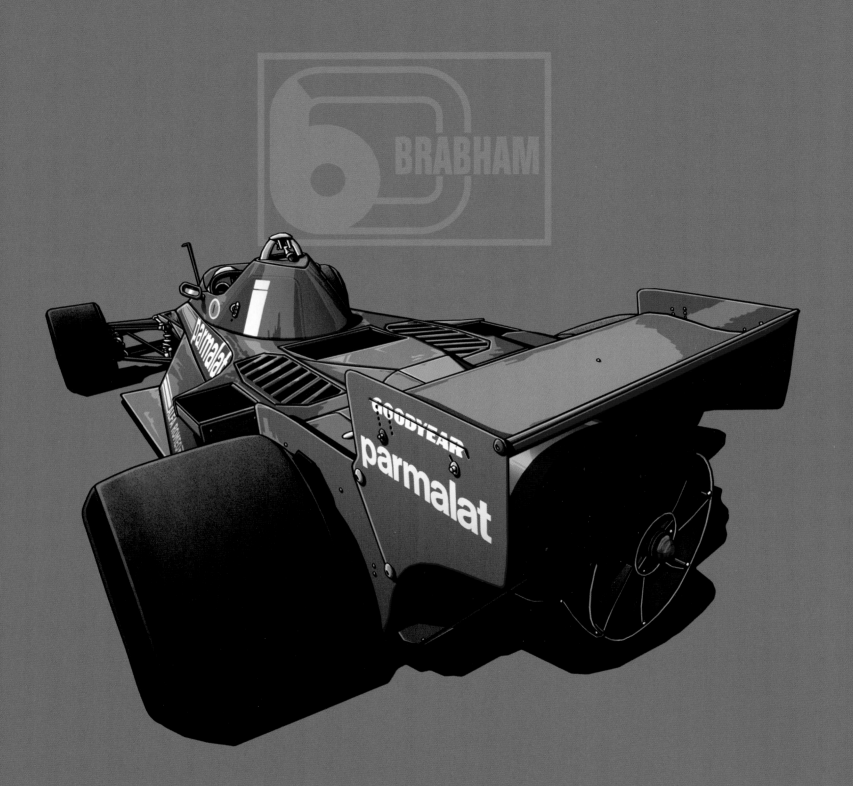

BRABHAM BT46B

"FAN CAR"

Every Formula 1 team dreams of the elusive one-hundred-percent success rate. A win at every outing—it's a cinch, surely? Forget the competition! In 1978, the Brabham BT46B reigned supreme when Niki Lauda surpassed all rivals in the debut race at the Swedish Grand Prix. Thereafter, the Brabham never won a race. In fact, it never raced again. The BT46B was a unique F1 car. Designer Gordon Murray felt he had to one-up Lotus with their superior "ground effect cars." He borrowed an idea from sports car manufacturer Chaparral, whose models were fitted with two large fans, designed to draw air from beneath the car. That increases downforce, so the drivers can corner at higher speeds. Like on the Lotus, movable "skirts" sealed the gap between the car's sides and the ground. Even in qualifying, drivers on its tail complained of sand and gravel that Brabham's "Fan Car" sprayed in its wake. The official claim that the fan was part of the engine cooling system proved untenable after the win in Sweden. The design was banned after rival teams questioned its legality. Gordon Murray, the legendary Formula 1 designer, had to come up with another innovation. Lotus was also obliged to abandon a similar concept.

1978	3.000 CC	400 HP	N/A

BUGATTI TYPE 32

"TANK"

Back in 1923, the press soon coined a nickname when the Bugatti Type 32 entered the race circuit. Motoring journalists at the track described the bizarre-looking vehicle from Molsheim as the "Tank de Tours." Its design radically departed from other racing cars with its rounded nose, sharply tapered tail, and flat sides at right angles to its front and rear wheels set into the bodywork, yet without the familiar full exposure to airflow. Ducts for engine air supply and ventilation covered the entire body. There was a smidgen of an oversized-soapbox look. However, the Bugatti team had discovered that racing cars are affected by aerodynamics, plus the Type 32 was a styling one-off. With a top speed of 120 mph (190 km/h), despite a power output of only 80 hp, the effect of reduced air resistance was evident. This racing car from Alsace underperformed on its first outing and finished third in its only entry in the 1923 French Grand Prix. The Bugatti, painted in traditional blue uniform, never entered another race. The reasons are unclear. Another Bugatti "Tank" racer, Type 57G, appeared in 1936. Its tank-bodied form was more aerodynamic and elegant than the Type 32.

1923	1.991 CC	80 HP	120 MPH

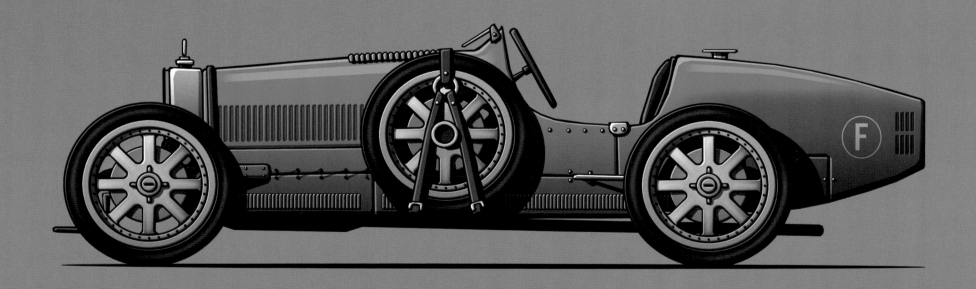

BUGATTI TYPE 54

"WIDOW MAKER"

1,000 wins! The Bugatti Type 35 enjoyed an almost incredible run of victories in the 1920s. Drivers like René Dreyfus or Louis Chiron won legendary events like the Targa Florio and the Mille Miglia. At just 2.3 liters and producing 130 hp, the straight eight-cylinder engine reached its limits against ever tougher competition. In 1931, Ettore Bugatti decided to risk everything on one card; he fitted a 5.0-liter, eight-cylinder engine behind the characteristic horseshoe grille. The supercharged engine developed 300 hp, although a methanol fuel mix would increase that to an incredible 450 hp. Many factors worked for the Bugatti Type 54. Yet, it only managed a single third place in 1931, at the Gran Premio di Monza. The car banked two wins during the next season, in the hill climb at La Turbie and the AVUS race in Berlin. Its unsavory reputation emerged due to its challenging drive and massive power. Few drivers could handle it. Count Czaykowski and Georg Christian, Prince of Lobkowicz, tragically lost their lives in a Type 54. British journalists gave the car the ominous nickname "Widow Maker." Although the Type 54 failed dismally when compared with the Type 35, its exotic styling made it a notable, pared down pre-war racing car that was a design template for the time.

1931	4.972 CC	300-450 HP	125 KM/H

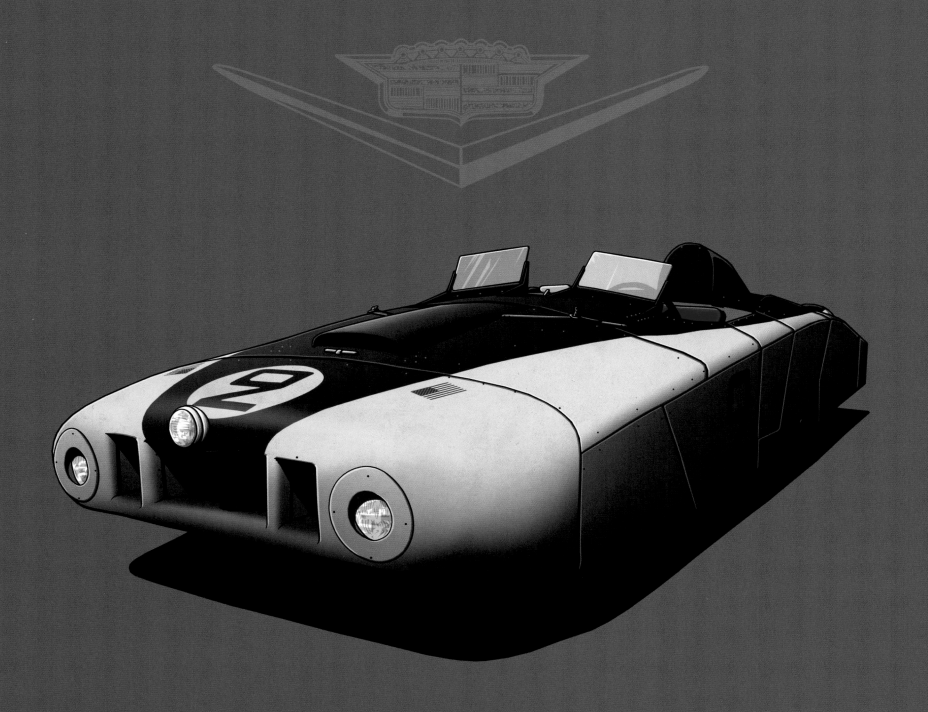

CADILLAC SERIES 61

"MONSTER"

When the crowd names a car "Le Monstre"/"Monster," it must be because of its gruesome appearance. Take one look at the Cadillac Series 61 and you can instantly appreciate this. The rule-defying open racing car was ultra-flat. None of its four wheels was exposed; it had two widely spaced eyes, and in-between, the ravenous jaws of an air intake. Hopes were faint of this design ever winning a Concours d'Elegance. But that wasn't the point. The challenge was to win the 24 Hours of Le Mans in 1950. Briggs Cunningham, a US racing driver and constructor, rose to this challenge. He entered two vehicles for the classic endurance race at La Sarthe, and a Cadillac Coupé de Ville was the technical basis for the "Monster." Aircraft design experts at Grumman Aircraft added the aerodynamic outer skin. Sadly, their efforts never paid off. In the second lap, a driver error put the "Monster" in a gravel trap at Mulsanne. The recovery operation lasted twenty minutes, so the US racer was in 35th place toward the back of the pack. Cunningham and his co-driver Phil Walters drove the remaining 23 hours and 40 minutes, finishing the race in 11th position. The "Monster" won kudos from its rivals and the media.

1950	N/A	N/A	N/A

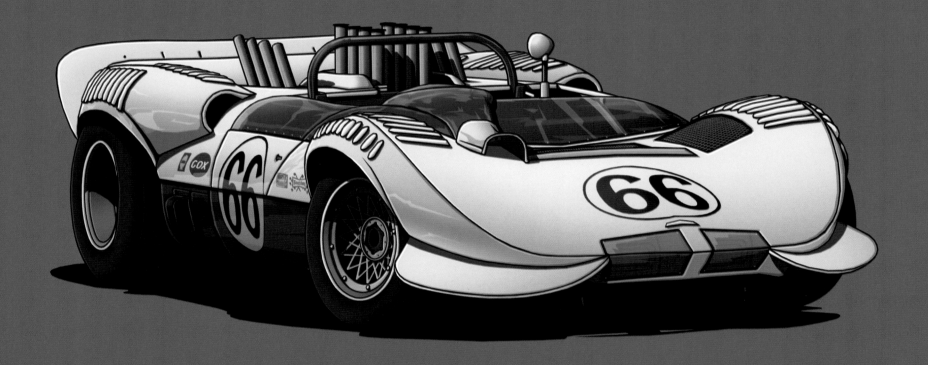

CHAPARRAL 2C

"EYE BALL JIGGLER"

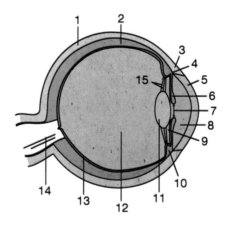

Look closely to find several pioneering aerodynamic properties on the Chaparral 2C. For example, the low front spoiler contributing downforce on the front axle. Add to that a driver-controlled wing on the rear spoiler for more downforce or to increase the top speed. Jim Hall, the Texan racing driver and constructor, gave the two-seater several ducts in the wheel wells, so air accelerated by the wheels could exit faster to reduce drag. Trackside fans loved the bloodcurdling howl of its 5.4-liter V8 engine. After the 1964 race at Laguna Seca, Jim Hall combined the Chevy engine with an automatic gearbox, keeping the driver's left foot off the pedal for braking or adjusting the rear wing, while the right foot operated the throttle. Groundbreaking innovations certainly tested the rival teams. Jim Hall and Hap Sharp scored an amazing win in 1965 in the 12 Hours of Sebring race. The nickname "Eye Ball Jiggler" originates from the experimental bodywork. Instead of fiberglass, the car's riveted aluminum structure produced such extreme vibration that the Chaparral 2C driver had difficulty staying focused on the race circuit.

1963-1965	5.356 CC	475 HP	N/A

CHAPARRAL 2H

"GREAT WHITE WHALE"

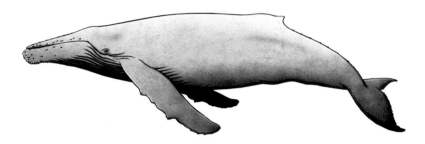

Mid-1960s innovations with the Chaparral 2 to 2C models culminated in the 2H in 1969. Co-founder Jim Hall, making a design turnabout, chose a fully enclosed shell for the 2H, rather than ever more downforce and monstrous wings. Its streamlined shape was for the lowest possible wind resistance. Competitors called it the "Great White Whale" due to its sleek exterior and long, narrow form. The Chaparral 2C to 2G's adjustable wings were history, since they'd been banned by a change in the FIA regulations. This car was disappointing. Out of four races, it achieved a single fourth. Hall and his team predicted better lap times than the car's potential delivered. Speed advantage couldn't compensate for the loss of downforce when cornering. Besides, there were issues with the dramatic chassis design. The world's first entirely fiberglass monocoque soon began to crack and had to be reinforced. A severe crash, which left Jim Hall in a wheelchair for a long while, left him unfit to test the 2H. Hall hired British Formula 1 World Champion and CanAm Champion John Surtees, who felt uneasy in the 2H, and refused to race again in the "Great White Whale."

1969	7.046 CC	650 HP	N/A

CHAPARRAL 2J

"SUCKER CAR"

Jim Hall devised another technical innovation for the 1970 motorsport season: the Chaparral 2J, the most extreme racing car of its time, and with its most innovative shape yet. Its revolutionary design was an angular box with fully enclosed rear wheels and two huge fans at the back. Hall's idea was "ground effect" which added maximum downforce by means of a vacuum. The vacuum was created by a two-stroke engine from a snowmobile. It ran continuously at 5,000 rpm and suction evacuated air from under the car. It was no surprise that the Chaparral 2J was called the "Sucker Car." Articulated Lexan polycarbonate skirts sealed the sides and rear against the ground. Hall's flash of genius worked—the bizarre box piloted by Vic Elford frequently secured pole position in qualifying. Yet, under race conditions the fan motor failed more often than its creator would have liked. Rival teams eyed it mistrustfully, claiming its basis was a movable aerodynamic device. They tried to outlaw the "Sucker car." Disillusioned, Jim Hall withdrew from motorsport at the end of 1970. Eight years later, the vacuum concept reared its head again in Formula 1. In 1978, Gordon Murray copied the Chaparral 2J and used a rear-mounted fan in his BT46B ground effect racing car—until Formula 1 rules also banned the concept.

1970	7.620 CC	680 HP	N/A

CHAPARRAL 2K

"YELLOW SUBMARINE"

Chaparral co-founder Jim Hall was still flirting with motorsport after his withdrawal in late 1970. He supported Canada's Brian Redmann in CanAm Racing, and quietly pursued his personal comeback. This time, he concentrated on IndyCar racing. Impressed by Colin Chapman's Lotus 78, the first Formula 1 car to use ground effects, Hall tasked British designer John Barnard with creating a similar single-seater for the legendary Indianapolis 500. The 1979 Chaparral 2K also used aerodynamic tricks: a negative wing profile over the side pods, sliding skirts on the underside of the car adding downforce, and higher cornering speeds than traditional cars. Driver Al Unser Sr. was keen to repeat his 1978 IndyCar win. After taking pole position soon after the start, he dropped back due to transmission issues. The 2K's "Yellow Submarine" moniker—thanks to sponsor, Pennzoil's corporate yellow paint scheme—showed its superiority several times during the 1979 season. It only scored its first win in the final race at Phoenix International Raceway. In 1980, the 2K won five out of its twelve races, powered by a 780 hp Cosworth V8 turbo engine. Its superiority ended in 1981 when other ground effects cars joined the grid. In 1982, Jim Hall stepped back again from motorsport racing.

1979-1981	2.643 CC	780 HP	N/A

CHEVROLET 150

"BLACK WIDOW"

Those who mourn the passing of this "Black Widow" can only blame themselves. The Chevrolet 150's legacy is connected to two men who had been let down, even side-lined, until they said to themselves, "It's now or never." Bradley Dennis and Paul McDuffie were driving for the SEDCO team in the mid-1950s, when Chevrolet pulled the plug. To make a long story short, the pair founded the Atlanta Tune Up Service. Chevrolet still supplied them with vehicles. Yet, as Bradley Dennis recalled, "Chevrolet sent us the cheapest cars they could, to make race cars out of them." The duo set to work, persuading some top racing drivers of the day to drive for them. GM soon noticed, and created the Stock Car Competition Guide in 1957. The paint scheme for all "Black Widow" cars was exclusively black and white. There are questions over the numbers of "Black Widows" built, or how many were still under construction. No verifiable figures are available, because the "Black Widow" never officially rolled off the Chevrolet production lines.

1957	4.638 CC	283 HP	N/A

CHEVROLET 3100 PICK UP

"BUBBLE MAKER"

A pickup in true American style—genuine, pure Detroit iron—well known to many and notorious to some. Nothing on wheels with a flatbed or load area ever had a reputation for pussyfooting around, making the nickname for the Chevrolet 3100 pickup so surprising: "Bubble Maker." While its competitors could cause an earthquake with their deep, guttural exhaust tones, the 3100 was comparatively quiet and reserved for the post-war period. At least, to American ears. By modern European standards, however, even the six-cylinder engine of the "Bubble Maker" throbs. How did the Americans come up with the idea of something as benign as a soap bubble? Well, when a serious V8 rolls up, this truck seems so quiet by comparison, it's like the quiet sound of a bubble maker.

1947-1955	3.859 CC	123 HP	N/A

CHEVROLET

CHEVROLET CORVETTE

"VETTE"

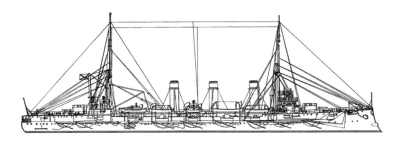

Just imagine it—one of the two all-time successful sports cars beginning life as a slow burner? Not only the lousy sales figures confirm this in the Corvette's early 1953 production run, but also several late 1950s pictures taken by former celebrity photographer Edward Quinn. International film stars graced the photos of famous brands including Alfa Romeo, Austin Healey, Jaguar... but no Corvette. It all revolved around the engine. Producing 150 SAE-hp, this sports car was considered a quirky, eccentric freak with its distinctive British roadster body that was no match for powerful, modern American limos. By 1955, with a V8-engine-upgrade—not its straight-six—it was finally fitted with a more typical US motor that took it up to 360 hp. The Corvette's mission was to conquer the world and to make its mark, thus justifying it being named after the "Corvette," a small type of maneuverable warship. The story goes that when General Motors sought a new name for the sports car, a company insider came up with "Corvette" after paging through a dictionary.

1953-1962	5.354 CC	360 HP	150 MPH

6827 TM 75

CITROËN DS

"GODDESS"

Hitting upon the right word for this car was quite something. Shortly after its introduction in 1955, tester Alexander Spoerl, writing for *Der Spiegel* magazine, said, "It's not the car of the future, it's just the car of today. And everything else is a car of ... yesterday." This car's status was revolutionary back then—and that's a fact. The artist, Flaminio Bertoni, produced the concept drawing transposing pure avant-garde onto paper (sadly, he is often confused with the Italian car designer, Bertone.) But let's not forget the mid-1950s technology of cable-operated cornering lights! Nor its stable lightweight construction, plus a hydro-pneumatic chassis with gas-filled sphere elements that offered ride comfort, rarely equaled today. In French, the abbreviation "DS" is a word-play on "déesse," or "Goddess" in English. That beauty carried Citroën into a new era, selling more than any other large executive cars over a 20-year period. Citroën recently resurrected the name, reiterating its avant-garde brand credentials.

1955-1975	2.347 CC	130 HP	115 MPH

CITROËN TRACTION AVANT

"GANGSTER LIMOUSINE"

Would Bonnie and Clyde still be alive today if they had driven a Citroën 11CV Traction Avant, not a Ford V8, as their getaway car? It's pure speculation. The partners-in-crime from the early 20th century would now be well beyond their centenary years. But back in 1934, they could have survived longer than their early-to-mid-twenties, because that same year that they were gunned down inside a Ford V8 happened to coincide with the build of the Citroën Traction Avant. Soon, this car was commonly named the "Gangster Limousine" with its grip on the road being due to its front wheel drive, double wishbone, and torsion bar suspension at the front, as well as the solid rear axle. The groundbreaking technical system of the front wheel drive—enabling fast cornering and great escapes—inspired this Citroën's popular name. The "Gangster Limousine's" design duo, André Lefèbvre and Flaminio Bertoni, were also responsible for its successor in 1955: The Citroën DS.

1934-1957	2.866 CC	80 HP	90 MPH

DATSUN 240Z

"BIG SAM"

Not exactly a roaring success in Germany (where sales only totaled 303 cars), the Datsun 240Z still enjoyed a reputation as one of the shapeliest coupés ever made in Japan. Only insiders were privileged to know of its real brainchild, the German designer Albrecht Graf von Goertz. Its long hood was reminiscent of the Jaguar E-Type; the original, 240Z version was produced from 1969 to 1974, followed by the 260Z in 1975. The last of the range was called the 280Z and rolled off production lines between 1979 and 1984. The straight-six two-seater became a permanent fixture in motorsport too, as "Big Sam" proved. This racing Datsun had several incarnations. The first version was based on a works rally car: it entered the RAC rally in 1970 but had to retire early due to a crash. Another accident-damaged 240Z was combined with the original 1970 version in 1972. In the 1974 British Automobile Racing Club race, "Big Sam" managed to hold at bay the pack of Porsches and TVRs in the 3-liter class. Its name, "Big Sam," is down to its constructor, Spike Anderson. The Briton had previously built a car for hill climbing and had affectionately labeled it "Sam." The significantly wider Datsun 240Z just had to be "Big Sam."

1970	2.423 CC	245 HP	N/A

DATSUN 240Z

"SUGAR SCOOP"

The Datsun 240Z was known as the "Sugar Scoop," due to its distinctive headlamp cutouts. The cute nickname sharply contrasts with the rugged appearance of this Japanese coupé; any car that can twice win the East African Safari Classic Rally must qualify with a certain endurance level. In hindsight, the race across the African continent was the epitome of utter hardship. Extremely long special stages across the African veldt, across desert sands and gravel, coupled with the unbearable heat, punished men and machines to their limits. The high retirement rate was no surprise. Whoever finished ahead would have destiny on his side. After all, where better to prove that a car was fast and reliable, if not here? Datsun entered the Safari Rally several times. The 240Z took the lead for the first time in 1971, with Shekhar Mehta securing the second victory for the red-and-white coupé in 1973. The Kenyan was the most successful competitor ever, recording a total of five wins. Roland Gumpert, director of Audi Sport, said: "You could win that rally in a taxi, you just need Shekhar Mehta at the wheel." The East African Coronation Safari was first held in 1953 in celebration of Queen Elizabeth II's coronation. It was a fixed part of the World Rally Championship from 1972 to 2002, starting and finishing in Nairobi, Kenya.

1971-1973	2.497 CC	225 HP	N/A

DELOREAN DMC-12

"TIME MACHINE"

The DeLorean's auspicious future was on the silver screen. The trilogy of *Back to the Future* movies is accepted as cult viewing. Back in the 1980s, Marty McFly was traveling fast-forward to October 21, 2015, while Doc Emmet Brown opted for a DeLorean DMC-12 as his vehicle of choice. A 1980s' time machine model had to accelerate to 85 mph (140 km/h), so we're talking sports car. One with a stainless-steel body—plus gullwing doors—it gets better! The original screenplay had not penciled in a DeLorean time machine vehicle; the writers wanted a refrigerator, but director Robert Zemeckis and producer Steven Spielberg overruled, to avoid potential accidents with kids climbing into fridges and being trapped. Designed by Giorgetto Giugiaro, for various reasons, the DeLorean never equaled its movie-star success. Part of the pressing machinery for the steel panels ended up in the Atlantic as ballast for a fish farm off the Irish coast.

1981-1982	2.849 CC	132 HP	125 MPH

DODGE CHARGER DAYTONA

"WINGED WARRIOR"

In the 1960s, Formula 1 constructors understood the importance of automobile aerodynamics. A few years later, American racing car designers had to play catch-up. As usual, they didn't do things by halves. Chrysler Corporation's muscle cars, built in Motown Detroit, enthused the fans and critics with their enormous rear wings. "Winged Warriors" was the nickname for these two-door racing cars. The model's upgrade then added more aerodynamically rounded or pointed noses at the front. Fitted with meaty eight-cylinder engines up to 7.2 liters, the Dodge Charger could hold its own in mega showdowns on the banked superspeedway ovals. Unfortunately, the fans didn't have long to enjoy the winged warriors from Dodge, Plymouth, Ford, and Mercury: The new rules about their high speeds pulled the plug on the racing cars; they were banned in 1971. Buddy Baker, in his Dodge Charger Daytona, was the first racing driver in NASCAR history to break through the magic barrier of 200 mph (322 km/h.)

1969	7.210 CC	N/A	N/A

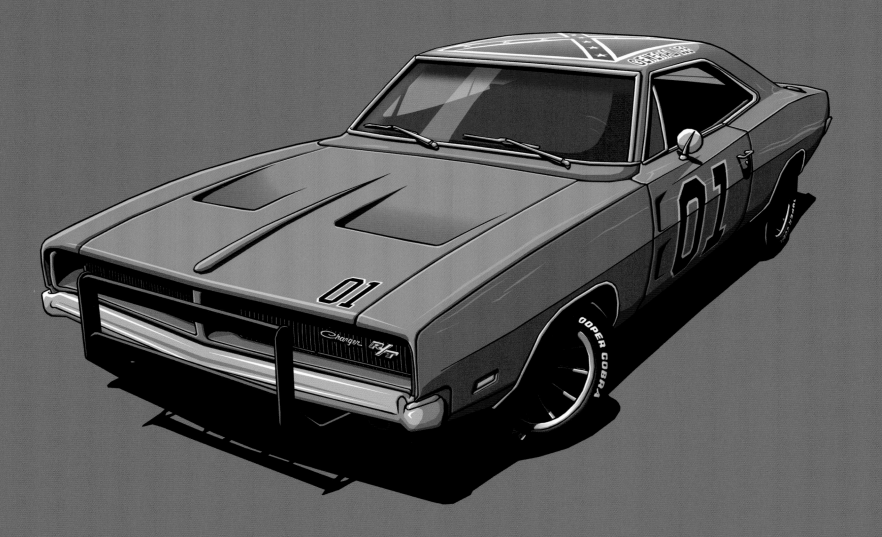

DODGE CHARGER R/T

"GENERAL LEE"

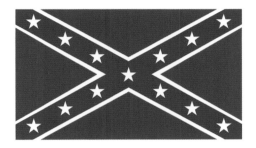

Wide, angular, loud, and orange, with "01" on the doors, naturally welded shut, and with a Confederate flag on the roof. That's what a Dodge Charger R/T ought to look like. Then, you can respectfully call it "General Lee." This Charger played the lead in the cult American TV series, *The Dukes of Hazzard*. Nobody was surprised that it suffered collateral damage from its spectacular stunts in legandary car chases. Allegedly, roughly 255 to 320 models, which were built in 1968 and 1969, were used during filming. (The 1970 model only featured in the 2005 cinema film.) Information is sketchy; however, 17 examples still exist in various states of repair. The jumps always caused the car plenty of problems, because the heavy engine in the front repeatedly tilted the nose of the car downwards when it was airborne. The stunt team tried to counteract this with sandbags in the trunk. "We enjoyed the jumps, but hated the landings," said a stunt driver. The Charger still helped the series achieve its cult status.

1968-1969	6.286 CC	330 HP	125 MPH

DODGE MONACO

"BLUESMOBILE"

The "Bluesmobile" is out of this world! It's got enough gas in the tank to drive through the night to Chicago, never mind the cigarette lighter. The 1974 Dodge Monaco, better known as the Blues Brothers' "Bluesmobile," was Dodge's flagship model in its day. Although automotive pundits and economists are unanimous about the Dodge Monaco being launched at the wrong time—this 7.2-liter V8 cop car coincided with the world oil crisis—die-hard fans know that it couldn't have emerged at a better time. The Dodge Monaco never wanted to be one of those classics that see motoring enthusiasts fall to their knees in awe, and gently cruise from show to show. It's no sculpture with glossy paint finish. The Dodge Monaco is smoky and throaty like the murky air in a downtown bar, a rough diamond on wheels with manners like a horde of wild animals, or in the words of the film's hero Elwood, "It's got cop tires, cop suspension, cop shocks."

1974	7.200 CC	280 HP	N/A

DUESENBERG SJ 12

"MORMON METEOR"

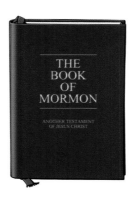

In the first decade of the 20th Century, Fritz and August Düsenberg from Lemgo in Westphalia, Germany, set up the Duesenberg Motor Company (DMC). They turned it into a prestigious car maker. In 1885, the brothers had arrived in Iowa with their mother who changed the umlaut in the family name to the Americanized Duesenberg. In the 1920s, Duesenberg cars achieved spectacular records and victories at Indianapolis and Le Mans. Thanks to their advanced technology, Duesenberg's models were popular with their discerning clientele, because DOHC engines and superchargers ranked them among the speedsters of their time. The Duesenberg SJ developed 320 hp with an incredible top speed of 165 mph (243 km/h). The 1936 record-breaking "Mormon Meteor" was based on the SJ. Just for once, it was not the public at large but a Salt Lake City newspaper—*Deseret News*—which invited its readers to name the special model. After all, it was powered by an airplane engine. The 25.7-liter V12 unit produced 750 hp at the rear wheels. It set new records over 24 and 48 hours.

1936	25.727 CC	750 HP	165 MPH

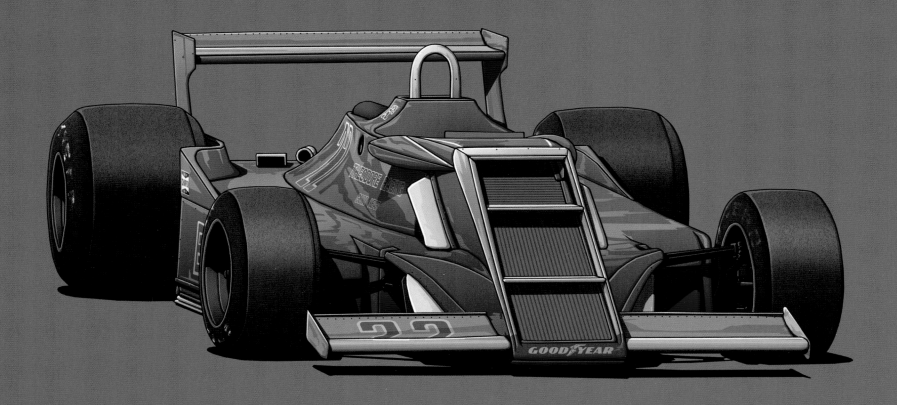

ENSIGN N179

"STEP LADDER"

Did you know…? The Ensign N179 had two nicknames. "Step Ladder" was thanks to its unorthodox front radiator grill. But designers and drivers had to endure uglier name-calling like "News Stand." True, there is an uncanny resemblance to a newspaper rack at a railroad kiosk. Yet, its drivers Derek Daly, Marc Surer, and Patrick Gaillard had to handle more than its weird appearance. The British F1 car was neither fast nor reliable. The N179 only attracted attention during the season for its repeated disappointments during race qualifiers. If it made it onto the grid, it was retired due to technical flaws or accidents. In 1979, the Ensign team's N179 chalked up not a single world championship point. The British racing team went down as one of least successful in F1's lengthy history. Even with well-known drivers at the wheel such as Nelson Piquet, Jacky Ickx, or Clay Regazzoni, they won nothing. The car's sole highlight was a fastest lap time by Switzerland's Marc Surer: in 1981, driving the successor model—Ensign N180B—he finished fourth in the Brazilian Grand Prix. Between 1973 and 1982, there were no more points finishes. This wasn't down to the engine, as many other manufacturers as well as Ensign relied on the Ford V8 Cosworth, or the DFV.

1979	2.993 CC	485 HP	N/A

FERRARI 250 GTB SWB

"BREADVAN"

British journalists soon dubbed this car the "Breadvan" because of its shape. Scuderia Serenissima Republica di Venezia—hired to provide the cars for the 1964 24 Hours of Le Mans—oversaw the conversion of this one-off from a normal 250 GT. Yet, the car was prohibited from showing a Ferrari emblem. The humorous name fit the assumption that the owner-designed sports car had next to no chance of finishing in the points. Nevertheless, successful designers Giotto Bizzarrini and Carlo Chiti were the real brains for the project. Both had left Ferrari following disputes. The car's eye-catching rear end Kamm tail design, housed another radiator behind a glass screen. But it was never needed: the Ferrari 250 GT "Breadvan" was forced to retire from the classic endurance race at La Sarthe when a driveshaft failed on the fourth lap. It was all over. The one-off racing car, which is still in private hands today, began a second career at classic car events. The Ferrari 250 GT "Breadvan" continues to appear at prestigious events, such as the Goodwood Festival of Speed in England, where Lord March happily presides over the participation of this unique build from Maranello, Italy.

1961	2.953 CC	292 HP	N/A

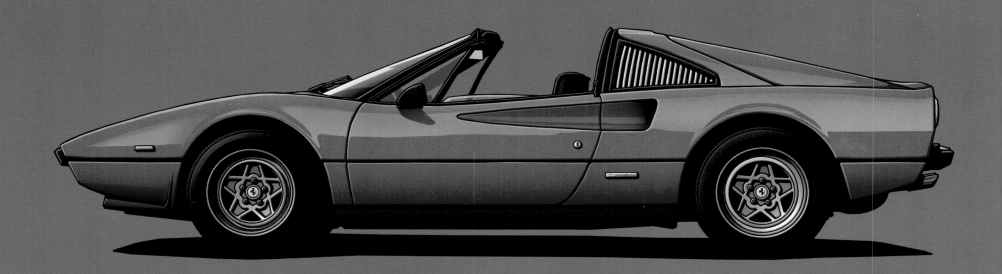

FERRARI 308 GTS

"MAGNUM"

First things first: this model is not Magnum's Ferrari. Aficionados know that the 308 GTS from the cult 1980s TV series *Magnum, p.i.* belonged to Robin Masters who, alongside his Ferrari, also made his entire estate available to Detective Thomas Magnum. What's more, the rumor is that Magnum actor Tom Selleck would have preferred a Porsche over a Ferrari, because the 308 GTS was designed for diminutive Italians rather than a tall American who was 6 ft 2 in (1.90 m). To accommodate Selleck, the seat had to be lowered and the steering column altered. The series rarely had shots of the roof, as Selleck barely fitted in the closed version. Various 308 GTS's were used, from the 1979 version to the 1984 GTSi QV, and they even retired a few; they came off worse in wild car chases, due to sporadic bullet holes and many accidents from fender benders to major crashes, even a bomb attack. Yet the Ferrari and Magnum remained inseparable. Ultimately, better Ferraris were available. Yet, no other model—except for maybe a white Testarossa in Miami—achieved its cult status.

1975-1985	2.925 CC	223 HP	155 MPH

FERRARI 365 GTB/4

"DAYTONA"

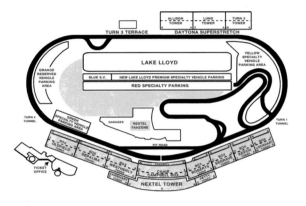

Nowadays, the Ferrari 365 range enjoys cult status. Different models have attracted various nicknames, some of greater renown than the official nomenclature. For example, "Queen Mary" for the GT 2+2, or "Il Gobbone" for the GTC/4. The "Daytona" for the GTB/4 is the most famous. The Spider GTS/4 "Daytona" achieved cult following with fans of US TV series *Miami Vice*. In black of course, although the film scenes included a McBurnie replica based on a Corvette, which presently enjoys its own cult status. The "Daytona" nickname started out as an unofficial designation that made it into the public domain. One last time, Enzo Ferrari asserted his liking for front-mounted engines in this 1969 car. The "Daytona" was never developed for competitive racing sport, it was far too heavy (3,527 lbs (1,600 kg), fully fueled, plus driver). A respectable 24 racing cars were built in total.

1971-1973	4.390 CC	352 HP	175 MPH

FERRARI F156

"SHARKNOSE"

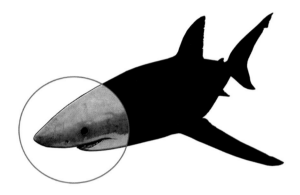

The roll call of drivers who have piloted this legendary Ferrari Formula 1 car reads like a contemporary Who's Who of motorsport: Hill, von Trips, Baghetti, Bandini, Gendebien, Ginther, Ireland, Mairesse, P. Rodríguez, R. Rodríguez, Scarfiotti, and Surtees. Of course, less glorious is the fatal accident of Wolfgang Berghe von Trips, whose life tragically ended in September 1961, when he was on the brink of his first World Championship victory. At Monza at the Italian Grand Prix, his F156 collided with Jim Clark's vehicle: it spun into the side barrier on the straight ahead of a banked curve, striking the wire spectator fencing and killing fifteen spectators. The incident is still referred to as "Formula 1's darkest hour." The 156 is dubbed "Sharknose" because of the shape of its front bodywork with the striking "nostril" air intakes. Ferrari celebrated the memory of this design some 40 years later with the F360 Modena production car and its successor, the F430.

1961-1964	1.476 CC	190 HP	N/A

FIAT S76

"BEAST OF TURIN"

Sometimes, all you need is a number: 28.4. That's the displacement—in liters—of the Fiat S76's engine. Next to this, even big block American monsters over 8 liters still seem like economical, green options. It gets more extreme when you discover that this 28.4-liter capacity comes from just four cylinders. Imagine the spit and growl of this animal when it was fired up! So musing on the origin of the S76 nickname is probably idle speculation. The "Beast of Turin" was built to break records, measurable in numbers, specifically the land speed record set by the Blitzen-Benz car at just over 125 mph (200 km/h). In 1911, the S76 stepped things up at 140 mph (225 km/h), making full use of its 290 hp—almost a ridiculous statistic by current standards. So much for published facts and figures. We're in the dark about one statistic: its fuel consumption. That's probably for the best in today's environment.

| 1911 | 28.353 CC | 290 HP | 140 MPH |

FIAT SB4

"MEPHISTOPHELES"

In the inter-war years, it was common to combine race cars with aircraft engines. Wealthy aristocrat drivers relished a contest for glory and the thrill of making new land speed records. The best way to boost engine performance was to increase engine capacity. That's what Briton Ernest Eldridge believed when he purchased the accident-damaged 1908 Fiat SB4 racing car. The 18 liter four-cylinder engine developed 175 hp, but that was too airy-fairy for him. He found a suitable replacement in the Fiat Type A12 engine: the straight-six engine developed 320 hp from just 22 liters and was originally fitted in a WW I fighter plane. After converting and altering the car, Eldridge headed for a country road near Paris in a bid for the record. In the Fiat, he achieved an average speed of 145 mph (235 km/h). Bystanders and journalists were so impressed by the infernal roar that they named the Italian racer "Mephistopheles." This name was the right match—Mephistopheles was the demon to whom Dr. Faust sold his soul. The Fiat with the airplane engine must have seemed like a hell-raiser to those close by. Unlike many land speed record cars of that era, the "Mephistopheles" has been kept for posterity: It has a place in the official Fiat collection and appears at exclusive classic car events-making a hellish impression every time.

1923	21.700 CC	320 HP	145 MPH

FORD ESCORT RS 2000

"DOGBONE"

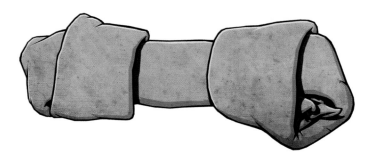

Escort Mark 1 was launched in 1967. Initially built for the British market, its nickname makes sense upon closer inspection. The radiator grille shape with typical narrowing between the headlights is reminiscent of one thing. Maybe the chief designer was a dog owner? This compact model was first assembled only at Ford's Halewood plant in England, though production was later extended to Genk in Belgium and the new factory in Saarlouis, Germany. Yet, the Escort was unpopular in Germany due to its bizarre appearance. Things were very different in Great Britain and in the motorsport world. The rear-wheel drive car was also available in a sporty RS version, making it the ideal basis for time trials on hard and loose surfaces. The RS 1600 and RS 2000 models notably made it onto the podium between 1973 and 1975. A popular saying in Britain was that "Every weekend, somewhere an event will be won by an Escort." Unfortunately, top racing drivers like Hannu Mikkola and many anonymous drivers, wore out so many of the RS 1600s, only 1,200 of which were ever built. The rare model, developing up to 270 hp, is now considered one of the most valuable Escorts ever made.

1967-1974	1.601-1.975 CC	100-270 HP	110-145 MPH

FORD GT MARK IV

"GT40"

What a comeback! In 1957, Ford had withdrawn from works motorsport. Company president, Henry Ford II, wanted to return to the race track in the early 1960s to enthuse younger customers for the brand. Le Mans and Indianapolis worked wonders to win over public opinion. But Ford lacked a car to rival the elite teams. One option was to buy Ferrari in its entirety. But wrangling ensued with Commendatore Enzo Ferrari, and the deal collapsed. Henry Ford II again backed off, but in a fit of pique told his engineers to create a Ferrari-beating vehicle. They developed the GT sports car, or the "GT40", alluding to its overall height of only 40 inches (1.02 m). Yet the low, mid-engine two seater still didn't win in 1964, at its Le Mans debut. All three works cars retired overnight with technical problems. Ferrari achieved three consecutive wins (a bitter pill for Ford). Similar dilemmas happened the next year, but from 1966 to 1969, at least one Ford "GT40" was always on the podium. Satisfaction at last for Ford. Fifty years on, Ford was back at the endurance race to the west of Paris. The new Ford GT not only won the GTE Class, but also held the Ferrari 488 in check. Victory is sweet.

1964-1969	4.178-6.997 CC	335-557 HP	185-200 MPH

FORD MODEL T

"TIN LIZZY"

Ford's Model T marked several milestones. With more than 15 million produced, it was the world's most prolific car until 1972, when it was overtaken by the "Beetle." And that's despite the Model T only being manufactured until 1927. Production of this simply designed vehicle began in 1908, a good-as-gold little Lizzy for the modest budget. Although the Model T was available in a range of variants, with or without doors, as a tourer, a tractor or a runabout, its appearance always looked somewhat tinny, hence its nickname, "Tin Lizzy." Real sales success began when Henry Ford introduced assembly line production in 1914. Unlike the manual process used everywhere else, this reduced tolerances and increased quality, leading to faster, more efficient assembly. Ford was a pioneer who realized he could seriously reduce retail prices, making the Model T affordable to even more potential customers. His plan worked. Suddenly, the car was priced at only $370, instead of its previous $850. Sales grew incredibly, with up to 9,000 cars being built every day at one point. The Model T mobilized the entire United States, and enjoyed huge success all over the world. A third of all cars sold back then were "Tin Lizzies." And most of them were black. Everyone knows Henry Ford's famous statement, "Any customer can have a car painted any color that he wants, so long as it is black."

1908-1927	2.875 CC	20 HP	45 MPH

FORD MUSTANG

"PONY"

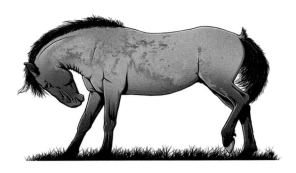

The Thunderbird was followed by the Mustang: US giant Ford had a real knack for hot sports coupés at that time. The Mustang's pleasing design was based on the Ford Falcon. The two-door car, initially available in coupé and cabriolet versions, created the "pony car" class, named after it. The Mustang enjoyed more success than its competitors, the Plymouth Barracuda and the Chevrolet Corvair. The attractive base price of just $2,400 and wide choice of optional extras and engines guaranteed high demand. The spiritual father of the Pony Car from Dearborn, Michigan was the legendary Car Guy, Lee Iacocca. During the eight years of the Series 1 production, Ford also built a few other models. The "Fastback" boosted sales, as did ever more powerful engines. The mighty Shelby versions were especially popular with customers looking for more horsepower. Racing driver Carroll Shelby created fast special editions—equally suited for the race circuit or the street. The Shelby GT-350 was launched in 1965, a rare and pricey model among Mustang fans. Ford is currently rediscovering the mythology of its past: The top model, known as the Shelby GT350, provides plenty of power from its eight cylinders and racing equipment. The Ford Mustang is still regarded as an American legend and is often mentioned in the same breath as Harley Davidson, Jeep and Corvette.

1964-1972	2.781-6.964 CC	101-390 HP	95-140 MPH

FORD TORINO TALLADEGA

"AERO WARRIOR"

"Aero Warrior"—it's not so much a nickname as a description for four muscle cars that were specially developed to compete in the 1969 and 1970 American NASCAR series. The 1969 Ford Torino Talladega, the first "Aero Warrior," was basically the only legitimate bearer of this name—*nota bene*, on the racing circuit. The Ford Torino Talladega did exactly what Ford anticipated: it won. To be precise, it scored 29 Grand National victories across the 1969 and 1970 NASCAR seasons. It also won the 1969 manufacturer's championship, and the driver's title too with David Pearson. When their competitors at Dodge realized that the Ford Torino Talladega's aerodynamics made it a much more effective racing car, they immediately went back to the drawing board and came up with the Dodge Charger Daytona. Strangely, that won at Talladega in 1969, while the Ford Torino Talladega won at Daytona.

1969	7.030 CC	600 HP	N/A

FUJI CABIN

"CYCLOPS"

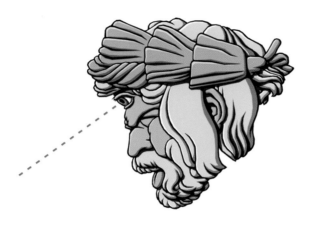

In hindsight, the years from 1953 to 1963 were exciting, at least in terms of design. Models during this era, which were developed for a generation of eager motorists, were quaint: the BMW Isetta, Messerschmitt Kabinenroller, and Zündapp Janus were the best known of these cars. But how do you define a car? Do three-wheeled vehicles count with only one headlamp on the nose? It was an exotic specimen, but the 1955 Fuji Cabin was conceptually like the German 'cars' of this age. A moped motor powered the car, while its bodywork kept the rain off the seat. When it was dark, there was a light at the front, just like any moped. That made it look rather like a "Cyclops," the one-eyed giant from Greek mythology. The steering wheel was no wheel; it was basically not round. The Cabin was steered using handlebars—it shared this in common with the Messerschmitt Kabinenroller. The engine was traditionally placed directly on the rear swing arm. In the case of the Fuji Cabin this was an air-cooled, two-stroke, single-cylinder engine, generating a whole 5 hp from its 122 cc. This made a potential maximum speed of 30 mph (45 km/h). Not exactly luxurious, but the population of a war-ravaged Japan was relieved to be on the road. Only 85 Japanese Cyclops models were built.

1955	122 CC	5,5 HP	30 MPH

GAZ M1

"BLACK RAVEN"

GAZ is the abbreviation for Gorkovsky Avtomobilny Zavod or the Gorky Automobile Factory. The M1 was launched in 1935, and although production was interrupted by the war, it was built until 1946. The M stands for Molotov. Vyacheslav Mikhailovich Molotov was then Chairman of the Council of People's Commissars in Russia. With almost 63,000 made, the GAZ M1 was the foremost car produced in Russia. In appearance, it was like contemporary vehicles from Ford—GAZ had been making Fords under license for some time. The public dubbed it the "Black Raven" ("Cherniy Voron", in Russian): the M1 was often driven by members of the much-feared NKVD (or People's Commissariat for Internal Affairs—basically the secret police in the USSR). They arrived in the middle of the night, arrested their suspects and drove them in the GAZ M1 directly to prison for interrogation. The superstitions of the Russian people clearly played a part in naming this car; the raven has always been associated with death and the underworld due to its black plumage and somber call. GAZ no longer builds cars today; its product line consists mainly of commercial vehicles.

1935-1946	3.285 CC	50 HP	60 MPH

GENERAL MOTORS LUNAR ROVING VEHICLE

"MOON BUGGY"

The "Moon Buggy" was the popular name for explorer vehicles to launch excursions on the lunar surface as part of the Apollo 15, 16, and 17 missions. Built by GM, its top speed of just 8 mph (13 km/h) was down to its specification as a mobility vehicle to facilitate scientific discoveries—its driver, James Irwin's mission was to record as much as possible, to take photos, and bring back lunar samples. But the Lunar Roving Vehicle had a bumpy start. When Irwin assembled the vehicle, he discovered that the steering on the front axle was not working. However, GM engineers had also fitted the "Moon Buggy" with rear axle steering, so the mission was not endangered. The lunar vehicle, developed in 1969, was made entirely of aluminum and had a dry weight of just 463 lbs (210 kg). It was driven by four 0.18 kW wheel-mounted electric motors. A 36-volt battery with a capacity of 121 amp hours gave it an active radius of 57 miles (92 km).

1969	N/A	0,9 HP	8 MPH

HONDA RA300

"HONDOLA"

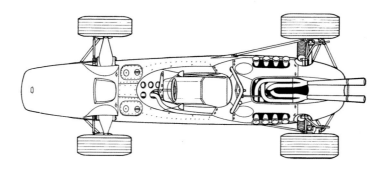

Honda and Formula 1—a double-edged sword. Compared with the success of the Japanese company's engine manufacturer division, the works Formula 1 team failed to live up to expectations. Honda made its debut in the premier racing category in 1964. A year later, a Honda RA 272 first crossed the line to victory. World champion John Surtees joined Honda in 1967. The Briton brought his expertise and attention to detail into play for the enthusiastic Japanese team. On his say-so, the RA 273 model, which had opened the racing, was swapped for the RA 300 mid-way through the season. It was unique because the RA 300 was built on a Lola chassis, leading to its nickname, "Hondola." This gamble paid off; on its debut at Monza, Surtees never gave the competition a chance. However, it only managed fourth place in the 1967 Constructors' Championship. Its successors in 1968, the RA 301 and RA 302 didn't win a single Grand Prix. By the season's end, the racing team had withdrawn from Formula 1. Honda celebrated its comeback in 1983, yet only as an engine manufacturer. Teaming up with McLaren gave Honda its greatest successes: 44 wins from 1988 to 1991, and four drivers' and four constructors' championship titles.

1967	2.992 CC	420 HP	220 MPH

S.S. JAGUAR 2 1/2 LITRE

"POOR MAN'S BENTLEY"

The company's founder, William Lyons, launched his first Jaguar in 1935, the S.S. 2.5 liter. It evoked up-to-date styling of the Bentleys, especially at the front, because large headlamps and the massive, vertical chrome grille were almost identical copies of the high-class original. This first Jaguar also won its nickname, "Poor Man's Bentley," because it was much cheaper to acquire. When William Lyons launched the car, he quizzed the attendees to estimate the retail price. The average guesstimate was £650. Prospective owners could buy into the six-cylinder car priced at £385—just over half the estimate. The 2.5 liter was more widely available to the public than any Bentley model. Incidentally, S.S. stood for "Swallow Sidecars". Founded in 1922, the company initially specialized in motorcycle sidecars. Later, it concentrated on building complete bodies at the Blackpool site for cars such as the much-loved Austin Seven. Understandably, the S.S. designation was dropped after the war. (English customers were unnerved by the S.S. label that had gruesome associations with the Nazi SS.). Henceforth, Jaguar became the established brand name, accompanied by the famous "Leaper", the elegant radiator mascot in the shape of a leaping spotted cat.

1935-1948	2.664 CC	104 HP	85 MPH

JAGUAR D-TYPE

"LONG NOSE"

Logically, you can't mention the C-Type without the D-Type. After victories for the Jaguar C-Type at Le Mans in 1951 and 1953, the Britons developed a worthy successor. The C-Type sports car was based on the XK 120 road-going sports car, while the D-Type was designed as a thoroughbred racing car. In 1954, the open two-seater with the striking rounded shape still had to follow in the wake of Ferrari, but nothing got past the Jaguar D-Type from 1955 to 1957. This run of successes led the brand with the feline mascot laying foundations for its leading international image. After 1955, all D-Types were known as "Long Nose," because the front of the car was extended by 7.5 in (19 cm) with the aim of increasing potential top speed at La Sarthe high speed circuit. The fin behind the driver were based on aerodynamic research, and drivers reported previously unprecedented stability under maximum load. The 3.4-liter, straight-six engine borrowed from the XK 120 was tuned to produce 250 hp, enabling the D-Type to reach 175 mph (280 km/h) on the long Mulsanne straight. This concept gave the lie to Enzo Ferrari's haughty claim that "Aerodynamics is for people who don't know how to build engines." No kidding! Sadly, however, Jaguar's effortless win at Le Mans in 1955, with the driver pairing of Mike Hawthorn and Ivor Bueb, was overshadowed by a terrible accident in which more than 80 spectators were killed.

1954-1957	3.442 CC	250 HP	175 MPH

JAGUAR E-TYPE

"ULTIMATE CAT"

The best-known Jaguar must be the E-Type. It's not surprising that the multi-award winning sports car was labelled the "Ultimate Cat." With its enchanting lines dominated by that never-ending hood, the E-Type is one of the most beautiful sports cars of all time, in the opinion of car fans all over the world. The 1961 Mk 1 coupé with narrow chrome bumpers and graceful lights, looked fantastic from any angle. The rich and beautiful people of the Swinging Sixties loved to be seen in the British two-door, which was also available as a cabriolet version. Fictional FBI agent Jerry Cotton even took the Jag on a manhunt, something that ensured long-term high demand, especially in the US market. Countless racing successes boosted sales still further. However, the original Jaguar form was gradually watered down over time. The 2+2 seater with a longer wheelbase, the Mk 2 and especially, the overblown-looking V12 model from the 3rd and final variant were further distanced from the archetype of the purist sports car. In the end, the "Ultimate Cat" was morphed into a comfortable cruiser, with the sweeping style of its successor, the XJS, providing a final separation from the mystique of the E-Type.

1961-1975	3.781-5.343 CC	265-276 HP	150-155 MPH

LAND ROVER S2A SAS

"PINK PANTHER"

The name may sound whimsical and amusing, yet its purpose was serious. The Land Rover Series IIA, known as the "Pink Panther," was a military utility vehicle used by the British Army's Special Air Service (SAS). The SAS is one of the most experienced and oldest special forces units still in existence today. The unit has its origins in the Second World War. Around 100 Land Rover Series IIA models were converted by the military, or developed from the ground up as a purebred military vehicle. Adaptations included compasses, machine guns, or extended range fuel tanks. For desert deployments, some models were painted pink as the best base color for camouflage in desert landscapes. Hence the name, "Pink Panther." Similar retro-fits were also made for the Defender. The SUV driven by professional footballer Franck Ribéry also sports pink paintwork. Is that a tribute to the "Pink Panther," or rather a gimmick from an eccentric player with the FC Bayern München soccer team?

1958-1971	N/A	N/A	N/A

LANSING BAGNALL RAPIDE ELECTRIC TRUCK

"LI'L TUGGIE"

If Lil Tuggie reminds you of an American rap artist with a small record label, it's because this is a rap musician. Hey, wait a second… His stage name seems to have been inspired by the colloquial term for this British-made electric forklift. That said, the Lansing Bagnall Rapide made it into this hall of fame because of its zany appearance and short-lived media career. In a 1970s episode of the British TV series "The Sweeney," Lil Tuggie features in a cameo role unloading cement sacks from a truck while the actors are deep in conversation. Lansing (then and now based in Basingstoke, England, and presently trading as Linde) was acquired in 1989, by German-based Linde Material Handling, which still makes forklifts and warehouse technology.

N/A	N/A	N/A	N/A

LOTUS 56

"DOOR STOP"

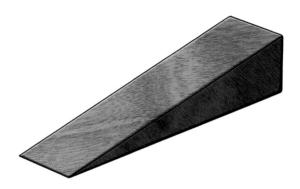

The Lotus 56 is a shining example of innovation potential in racing car design. Like the STP-Paxton Turbocar and the Shelby Turbine Indy Car, turbine power was meant to drive this single-seater onto the podium at the legendary 500-Mile Race at Indianapolis. Its Pratt & Whitney ST6 Turbine was developed for airplanes and helicopters. At a length of ca. 5 ft. (1.5 m), the Lotus engine is fitted directly behind, not close by the driver. The Lotus also has all-wheel drive to get its 550 hp on the road. "Door Stop" alludes to the car's extreme wedge shape with flat nose. Racing team owner Colin Chapman had two early setbacks with the Lotus 56. Firstly, Jim Clark suffered a fatal accident in a Formula 2 race in spring 1968. Then a month later, replacement driver Mike Spence died in a serious accident during qualifying at Indianapolis. Lotus subsequently entered Graham Hill, Joe Leonard, and Art Pollard. Leonard recorded the best qualifying time and gained pole position for the race. Rivals already had their doubts about the superiority of these turbo cars. Later, regulators had to bow to pressure from successful teams. Instead of kerosene, only regular gasoline was allowed as fuel. Leonard could still compensate for loss of performance, quickly taking the lead. Chapman's dire disappointment was that all three cars were compelled to retire.

1968	N/A	550 HP	N/A

LOTUS 79

"BLACK BEAUTY"

Black and gold—in the eyes of many fans, this is Formula 1's most beautiful color scheme. Chief sponsor, John Player Special, dictated the sleek design of British Lotus racing cars from 1973 to 1979. The Lotus 79 was unveiled in 1978—it was a logical progression from the '78, the first ground effects racing car. An inverted wing on the side pods and consistent seal from skirts ensured a clean exit for air flow under the car that could generate exceptional downforce. Cornering speeds rose strikingly. Fans dubbed the Lotus 79 "Black Beauty." During the 1979 season, rivalry among the teams was hardly on a level playing field—so superior was the Lotus wing car that other drivers may as well have been standing still. Mario Andretti and his team mate Ronnie Peterson, who was later killed in an accident in Italy, placed first and second in the world championship. Yet the British team failed to consolidate the victory. Competitors copied the wing car; they also refined its technology. Lotus began falling behind. Eventually, its decline could no longer be stopped. In late 1982, team founder Colin Chapman died of heart failure at age 54. Lotus still thrived in the turbo era, but lacked the charisma to win a world championship title.

1978	2.997 CC	480 HP	N/A

LOTUS CLIMAX 25

"BATHTUB"

Its monocoque structure made the Lotus 25 a total revolution in 1962. A brand-new, lightweight, rigid aluminum chassis design facilitated improved handling—an innovation in F1. The small 190-hp Coventry Climax engine—fitted behind the driver—was integrated into the monocoque body by means of a tubular frame. The only downside was that its design virtually pushed the driver into a reclined seating position, which explains the nickname "Bathtub." Scottish driving hero Jim Clark finished the first F1 season in second place, behind Graham Hill. It was almost a clean sweep in 1963: the pairing of Clark in the Lotus 25 won seven of ten races, taking both world championship titles. Colin Chapman's pioneering design genius now came to light. Rivals like Ferrari, BRM, and Brabham lagged behind with their use of almost exclusively outdated materials. Mid-way through the '64 season the Lotus team replaced the awesome Type 25 with its successor, the 33. Clark posted two further wins in the Lotus 25, but at the year-end, after several mechanical failures of the new 33, he ranked only third in the world championship. Lotus improved the car's rigidity over the winter and Clark resumed his run of successes in 1965, culminating in another decisive win of the drivers' and constructors' championship titles.

1962-1965	1.497 CC	190 HP	155 MPH

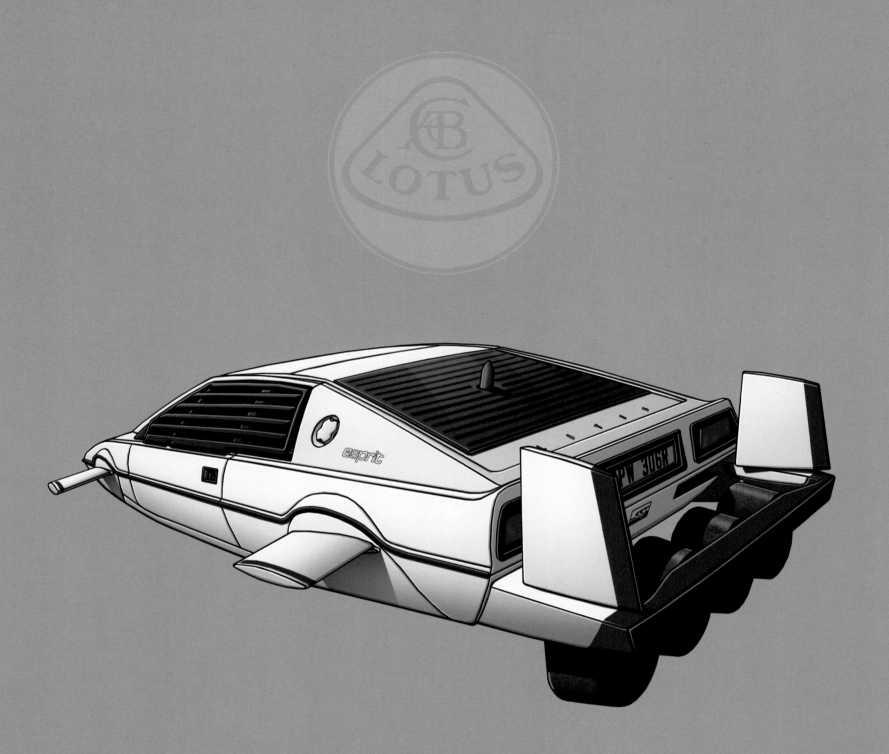

LOTUS ESPRIT

"SUBMARINE"

Despite a 30-year production heritage, only about 10,000 of these cars were made. This British sports car is one of the most famous movie classics of all time. Its starring role in the James Bond film *The Spy Who Loved Me* was a runaway success. Spectacular underwater scenes filmed in Sardinia caused a stir. As the mid-engined dolphin fled from the gunfire of a helicopter in hot pursuit, it plunged into the sea, metamorphozing into a submarine. Its wheels folded away, hydroplanes flipped out, and four rear propellers drove it through the water. The special effects team employed by producer Albert R. Broccoli surpassed expectations in this 1977 Bond film. Roger Moore reacted in character, with a phlegmatic raise of the eyebrow as the interior of the Lotus Esprit transformed into a real submarine. Co-pilot Barbara Bach rubbed her eyes in awe as the watertight sports car cruised serenely through the Mediterranean. Thanks to the technical genius of Q, the craft was also fitted with an anti-aircraft gun, giving the white submarine-in-Lotus-cladding the impact it needed. At the flick of a switch, Agent 007 scored a direct hit at the chopper hovering above the sea.

1976-2003	1.969-3.506 CC	150-354 HP	125-175 MPH

MASERATI TIPO 61

"BIRDCAGE"

Jaguar, Aston Martin, Ferrari, and Maserati—there was a time when all four auto makers went head to head for the sporting laurels. In 1959, Officine Alfieri Maserati S.p.A. presented a new design. The Tipo 60 with lightweight bodywork hid an unusual chassis; design chief Guido Alfieri had welded about 200 individual tubes into a tight lattice, hence the name "Birdcage." Maserati director Omer Orsi wasn't passionate about this solution, as other manufacturers had already embraced an aluminum monocoque. The four-cylinder, 2.0-liter engine was fitted at a 45-degree angle, which improved the aerodynamics. With dry sump lubrication, the engine could sit down low in the "Birdcage." Six Maserati Tipo 60s had been built, each one producing about 200 hp, when the Modena factory received an enquiry from the United States. With a 3-liter engine, the "Birdcage" would be able to enter races in the World Sports Car Series—and so the Tipo 61 was born, with a meager production run of 16 vehicles. The four-cylinder engine was bored out to 2.9 liters—the block couldn't take any more—with output at 250 hp. In 1960, the Maserati Birdcage won several races in the US and also in Europe: Stirling Moss and Dan Gurney won the 1,000-kilometer race (620 miles) at the Nürburgring in 1960. That triumph was repeated in 1961 with a driver pairing of Masten Gregory and Lloyd Casner.

1959-1960	1.989-2.890 CC	200-250 HP	175-185 MPH

MCLAREN M7A

"DOUBLE DECKER"

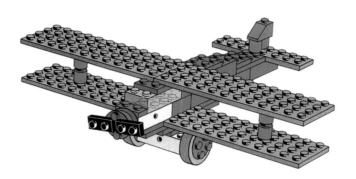

With a solid output of 400 hp from a 3-liter, eight-cylinder engine, the legendary Cosworth engine, or the DFV, made its Formula 1 debut in 1967. The V8 engine was initially exclusive to Lotus. Other teams gained access to it for the next season. That included McLaren. The newly developed M7A from the British racing team followed the trend for aluminum monocoque construction, with the engine structurally mounted at the rear. The M7A stormed ahead to its first race win, but it didn't count toward the F1 World Championship. In the car's second F1 race in 1968, Denis Hulme was runner-up. As the season advanced, the McLaren grew massive wings over front and rear axles—its designers had now grasped the importance of aerodynamics, making excellent use of increased down-force to boost cornering speeds. "Double Decker" was a buzz word: cars of its ilk raced at the pinnacle of motorsport. Team owner Bruce McLaren drove in the second M7A alongside Denis Hulme. He claimed his first victory in his own car at the fifth race of the season at Spa-Francorchamps. Having crossed the finish line, team director and driver McLaren was convinced that Jackie Stewart had stolen a win, having led for much of the race. The Scot's fuel ran dry on the final lap so McLaren only learned of his victory from his mechanics. "The best thing that I'd ever heard," said Bruce McLaren after his historic victory.

1968	2.993 CC	415 HP	N/A

MCLAREN M8D

"BATMOBILE"

Roughly 2 lbs (1 kg) per horsepower. Does that sound like a promising power/weight ratio? The McLaren M8D achieved an accurate 0.93 kg/hp. The two-seater racing car was born in the heyday of the CanadianAmerican Challenge Cup *aka* CanAm. Races were held exclusively in Canada and the US. An eight-cylinder Chevrolet engine was housed in a lightweight aluminum chassis. The huge V8 produced an almost monstrous roar with up to 680 hp, depending on its capacity variant, plus it weighed in at 1,398 lbs (634 kg). The "Batmobile" was nicknamed after the M8D's new aerodynamics. Unlike its predecessor, the M8B (the M8C didn't exist), the rear wing was no longer mounted high in the airflow but attached to two large fins at the sides. Such alterations paid off: Denis Hulme, Dan Gurney, and Peter Gethin won nine out of ten races in 1970, against rival cars from Lola, Porsche, and BRM. However, the papaya orange CanAm missile was also at the heart of a tragedy: team owner Bruce McLaren lost his life in an M8D. On June 2, 1970, he had taken the "Batmobile" to the Goodwood circuit for testing. At 170 mph (270 km/h), part of the rear bodywork broke loose, the car spun and struck a protective embankment. Bruce McLaren was thrown from the car and killed instantly.

1970	7.600 CC	680 HP	N/A

MERCEDES-BENZ 200 HP

"LIGHTNING BENZ"

At the turn of last century, the heat was on to develop ever faster speeds. In 1910, one of the most fascinating cars, the Mercedes-Benz 200 hp, made a grand entry on the international scene. Its design was based on that of the awesome 1908 Benz Grand Prix car. Technicians Victor Hemery, Hans Nibel, and their colleagues created an inspirational model that for the time being was the fastest car in the world with its whopper 21,500 cc inline four-cylinder engine. A full 200 hp guaranteed a thrilling drive. The most impressive evidence was the land speed record of 140 mph (228 km/h) set in 1911 by American Bob Burman over the flying mile at Daytona Beach—it remained unbroken until 1919. These record-breaking attempts were always run on sand. Considering the poor road surfaces and no windshields, then in comparison with today's standards, the performance commands respect for the audacious drivers. Early aerodynamic influences on vehicle design are evidenced in the impressive "Lightning Benz." American event manager Ernie Moross came up with the nickname; he dubbed the racing car the "Lighting Benz," because it was lightning fast.

1910	21.500 CC	200 HP	140 MPH

"FINTAIL"

The "Fintail Benz" models from the W 110/111/112 series are an exceptional phenomenon in the history of the Stuttgart automaker. For the first time, the design was inspired by transatlantic automotive trends, since tail fins on rear fenders were all the rage in the US. The Mercedes-Benz design team, headed by Karl Wilfert, couldn't resist this feature, although tail fins, which were known internally as "sight lines," were much less spectacular than those sported by many street cruisers. The official line was that they were a functional aid for reverse parking. Whatever the reason, the striking, chrome-trimmed corners of the car made this sedan famous and inspired its enduring name. Like its direct predecessor, the "Ponton," the W 110/111/112 was available as a long or short wheelbase variant, with four or six-cylinder engines. The six-cylinder was also fitted to the shorter car. The top-of-the-line model was the 300 SEL "Uber-Fintail" with 4-in (10 cm) longer wheelbase. Its three-liter straight-six engine with an output of 170 hp took the executive vehicle up to 125 mph (200 km/h). At the other end of the scale was the more pragmatic 55 hp 190 D "Diesel Fintail," the most popular taxi in Germany.

1959-1967	1.897-2.996 CC	55-170 HP	80-125 MPH

MERCEDES-BENZ W 113

"PAGODA"

They say that every Mercedes deserves a nickname. In the 1950s and 1960s, road-going cars were identifiable by their different epithets. The "Pagoda" described the Mercedes 230 SL. The new roadster replaced the 190 SL in 1963; it offered customers six rather than four cylinders. Its sober body design revealed no-frills styling that captivated the public with understated elegance and proved popular with high rollers. When its fabric convertible roof was folded down and a standard metal hardtop fitted, it was obvious why the SL had been named the "Pagoda." Its slightly concave hardtop was reminiscent of a style of pagoda roof, a distinctive Asian building shape. Yet, the SL was (and is) usually driven with its convertible roof down, so the remark—"See that Pagoda?"—is a misnomer. You just ain't gonna see that design-form. With the fabric cover closed, no concave center was visible either. Aside from these formalities the W 113, known as the SL, was a milestone in Mercedes tradition. In 1966, the 150 hp 230 SL was replaced by the equally powerful 250 SL. The follow-up in 1968 was the 280 SL with an output of 170 hp. The "Pagoda" also enjoyed success in motorsport—always the hardtop variant—in genuine pagoda style.

1963-1971	2.281-2.778 CC	150-170 HP	120-125 MPH

MERCEDES-BENZ W 196

"SILVER ARROW"

The 1934 Mercedes-Benz W 25 inspired the mythical status of the "Silver Arrow." The W 196 was the last, but hardly the least successful racing car of this line. The Stuttgart works team's drivers had the pick of two models: an open-wheeled single-seater and a fully enclosed, streamlined variant. Performance of the 2.5-liter straight eight-cylinder engine depended on the fuel load that contained varying mixtures of benzene, methanol, high octane gas, acetone, and nitrobenzene. In its most powerful incarnation, the Mercedes engine developed up to 290 hp, revving at up to 9,000 rpm. During the first outing at the French Grand Prix in Reims on July 4, 1954, Juan Manuel Fangio and Karl Kling dominated in their brand-new W 196s. Their competitors from Ferrari, Maserati, Giordini, and HWM had no chance and the duo achieved a sensational one-two win. That ushered in many more successes, including the unforgettable one-two-three win at the Berlin Avus by Kling, Fangio, and Herrmann. Nobody doubted the strength of the Mercedes-Benz works team. The miracle was complete in 1954, when Juan Manuel Fangio clinched the world championship title in the Mercedes-Benz W 196 "Silver Arrow."

1954	2.496 CC	257-290 HP	170-180 MPH

MERCEDES-BENZ 300 SL W 198

"GULLWING"

It was fast, elegant, expensive, rare, and spectacularly beautiful—an iconic Mercedes. The 300 SL is the German dream car *par excellence*. In 1954, the "Gullwing" showed the world that Germany had not forgotten how to build top-of-the-line cars with cutting edge technology. Only nine years after the end of the war and when Germany was in ruins, Mercedes restored faith in the country's car brands with one graceful vehicle. In technical terms, the southern German experts gave it everything they had: The tubular spaceframe chassis as launched two years previously on the 300 SL racing car to provide maximum stability, coupled with direct gas fuel injection for high power output. All this helped the 215 hp 300 SL reach speeds of up to 160 mph (260 km/h), depending on the rear axle configuration. At that time, an Opel Olympia could achieve a maximum of 75 mph (120 km/h). This sports car was beloved by the rich and famous people. In the US, the car was dubbed "Gullwing" because its opening doors were reminiscent of the wings of a seagull. Only 1,400 coupés were made, it was replaced in 1957 by the roadster, 1,858 of which were built. The Mercedes 300 SL sells for astronomical sums today.

1954-1957	2.996 CC	215 HP	160 MPH

MERCURY CYCLONE SPOILER II

"AERO WARRIOR"

"Aero Warrior" is a label for muscle cars developed especially for the NASCAR series in the late 1960s by Dodge, Plymouth, Ford, and Mercury. Initially, the models were based on ordinary production cars and later optimized by introducing more aerodynamic extras. The Mercury Cyclone Spoiler II was almost identical to the Ford Torino, only the front grille and tail lights made a visual difference. And just like its Ford brother, the Mercury created a real buzz on US race circuits: eight NASCAR wins in 1969 and 1970—all without any commercial backing. Some doubted whether the 500 cars required for homologation existed. Mercury claimed to have built 503 vehicles, but there were rumored to be just 351. At scheduled checks—with all 500 cars required for inspection—the rumor is that the numbers were made up by slipping in repainted regular "W" Cyclone Spoilers. That said, the Mercury earned its legitimate place among "Aero Warrior" legends on the race circuit.

1969	7.030 CC	600 HP	N/A

MEYERS MANX KIT CAR

"DUNE BUGGY"

Bruce Meyer loved the view of surfers, waves, and bikini-clad beauties. The artist, boat designer, and engineer soaked up the breeze and warmth by the Californian coast. Back in the Sixties, it was the norm for young dudes with souped-up V8 hot rods to leave their tracks across the sand, often grinding to a halt. When a Beetle chassis with no bodywork ran rings around the heavy hot rods, Meyer had a flash of genius: to create a design for a lightweight, attractive, fiberglass body. That's how the first featherweight buggy bodies were made in Meyer's workshop, where he already produced surfboards and boats from laminated fiberglass. A new genre of vehicle had been born: The "Dune Buggy." The Meyers Manx, named after the tailless breed of cat, was a kit car. Meyer sold only the parts, instructions, and a few accessories at very attractive prices. Demand was huge, the Californian "Dune Buggy" was the new kid on the block. Sadly, interest from copycats was also huge; they ripped off his idea and sold it themselves. He lost the resulting lawsuit. Eventually, the company folded in 1971. Meyer produced a Classic Manx in 2000, based on the original buggy and limited to a run of just 100. It was a happy ending for the inventor of the "Dune Buggy."

1964-1971	1.200-2.400 CC	34-120 HP	N/A

MGM GEN 11

"CHITTY CHITTY BANG BANG"

Chitty Bang Bang was the unofficial nickname for several supremely popular English racing cars dating from the 1920s. The designer and drivers were Louis Zborowski and his engineer, Clive Gallop. Worldwide publicity was courtesy of Ian Fleming, the spiritual father of James Bond. In Fleming's novel *Chitty Chitty Bang Bang: The Magical Car* the automotive protagonist suddenly appeared in the early 20th Century and was ready to steal victory at every outing before embarking on an epic adventure filled with twists and turns. A second Chitty was added and the car was equipped with useful functions like its flying mode. The famous movie car had little in common with the racing model, and of the six cars used in filming, only GEN 11 was registered for British road use. That car achieved a USD 805,000 price tag at auction in California in May 2011. Cue for more name-dropping. The buyer was none other than highly esteemed filmmaker with a passion for gripping tales and cars: Sir Peter Jackson, the brains behind films such as *Lord of the Rings*, the *Hobbit* trilogy, and *King Kong*.

N/A	N/A	N/A	N/A

MITSUBISHI LANCER 1600 GSR

"KING OF CARS"

The "King of Cars" label could be an exaggeration or royally deserved. Given the double wins posted by the Mitsubishi Lancer GSR 1600 at the Safari Rally Kenya in 1974 and 1976, its VIP accolade seems more than justified. Scoring a victory in the toughest, insanely brutal rally of its day—not once, but twice—is proof of stamina and talent. Just completing the race is tantamount to victory here. Dropout rates were about 25 percent. Then the Lancer joined in the race, the latest GSR 1600 model, to claim glory. With Joginder Singh at the wheel, it left a bevy of Nissan "Fairladys" and "Bluebirds" behind, pushing Björn Waldegård in a Porsche 911 into second place—despite the Porsche's one-liter bigger engine. Before long, the Lancer had booked its place in the hall of fame as the "King of Cars," and as the racing stalwart in Africa.

1974-1977	1.597 CC	171 HP	N/A

Plymouth

PLYMOUTH ROAD RUNNER SUPERBIRD

"WINGED WARRIOR"

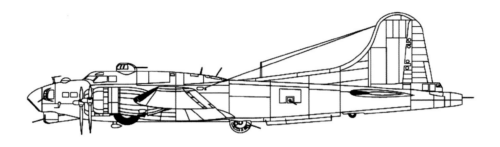

"Beep, beep!" That wasn't the horn of the 1970 Plymouth Superbird but it had plenty in common with the *Looney Tunes* cartoon hero Road Runner, a fast-running bird that first featured in *Fast and Furry-ous*. Even the car's unique design is reminiscent of the world's speediest bird. The rear spoiler stands out as its most striking feature. Frankly, what would a Road Runner be without a villain? In the case of the Plymouth, that role was filled by the Ford Torino Talladega, which achieved its own hero status as one of the four "Aero Warriors." In the Plymouth Superbird it had an arch rival, one which could accelerate from 0 to 60 mph in 5.5 seconds and—in ideal conditions—achieve a top speed of around 200 mph (320 km/h). The cult following of these very special racing cars is still as 'looney' as ever. It was immortalized in Pixar's 2006 film *Cars* in which "The King" appears in the original, genuine "Dinoco blue," the color of the most lucrative sponsor of the famous Piston Cup, a parody of NASCAR.

1970	6.980 CC	426 HP	200 MPH

PONTIAC

PONTIAC CATALINA

"SWISS CHEESE"

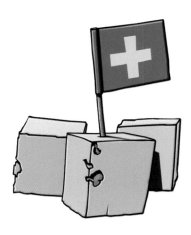

It may well be one of the oldest rules in lightweight car design, namely, "holes are weightless." In the early 1960s, Pontiac was the lead auto manufacturer for the NASCAR series and NHRA drag racers, although it was already obvious that the competition was gaining ground. The memo from the top was clear: get lighter and retain a competitive edge. So, 130 holes were drilled in the chassis for the 1963 season, which led to the nickname "Swiss Cheese." Steel components were swapped for aluminum and other weight reduction techniques were implemented, such as the removal of unnecessary parts because the rules stipulated that the racing car had to be made on the same production assembly line as the standard Pontiac. Ditto for the engine, which was officially a 405-hp 421 Super Duty. Tests showed that the engine developed much more power: one case recorded at 465 hp. That engine masterpiece, made with state-of-the-art materials, was installed after the car was built, but before shipping. The mechanics fitted it to just 14 vehicles.

1963	6.898 CC	405 HP	N/A

PONTIAC GTO

"THE GOAT"

John DeLorean was the inventor of the GTO. Yep, it was that DeLorean. He went on to devise the eponymous time machine for the *Back to the Future* trilogy. *Wunderkind* DeLorean unceremoniously appropriated the GTO designation for his performance car (for Pontiac) from the legendary Ferrari 250 GTO. Ferrari's GTO stands for Gran Turismo Omologato. Ferrari uses this designation for its homologated racing cars. Americans loved the high performance, yet inexpensive GTO. The nickname was more a cultural labor of love in that the "GTO" became known simply as the "Goat." (Apparently, most Americans find it easier to create the monosyllabic "goat" out of the tri-syllabic "GTO.") The vehicle was in high demand for quarter-mile drag racing, a popular event in the US. Its aura of powerful and gutsy bullishness gave its driver an unfair advantage over the competition, even before the starting lights went out. Its starring role as hero of the silver screen in many road movies was merely a logical consequence.

1965-1973	6.560 CC	355 HP	125 MPH

PORSCHE 356

"LADY"

Can you ever have enough power? Traditionally, women take a broader view of this issue than men. That's why the least-powerful 60 hp Porsche 356 was known as the "Lady." However, that wasn't the case from the start. The first production Porsche in 1950, produced only 40 hp from a 1.1-liter engine. The 356 justified Porsche's worldwide reputation, basing technical aspects on the VW Beetle and creating a desirable sports car. Over the course of its career, until 1965, the 356 was built in coupé, cabriolet and speedster versions, each more powerful than the last. Ultimately, the 60 hp variant took on the role of unpretentious entry model—the Porsche for the fairer sex. The other 356 versions developed more than twice the power, such as the 2000 GS from 1961, with its 130 hp four-cylinder boxer engine. Looking back, the 356 was the foundation for much of Porsche's success on race tracks all over the world. Its successor, the 911, to this day has remained true to the principle of the rear-mounted boxer engine. Since 2016, the 718 Boxster and Cayman models again use a four-cylinder boxer engine, just as the "Lady" once did, the 60 hp 356.

1955-1963	1.582 CC	60 HP	100 MPH

PORSCHE 550 SPYDER

"JAMES DEAN'S PORSCHE"

"Win on Sunday, sell on Monday." In the 1950s, the Porsche 550 Spyder proved the theory that wins on the race track boost sales. It worked particularly well in the American market. The 550 Spyder was the first real racing car from the Stuttgart brand and found success wherever it went. Its many victories made Porsche a household name in the United States. It was only natural that a very special owner should make this sports car a legend: Hollywood star James Dean raced his 550 Spyder in the US, and it was also at the wheel of this open two-seater that he met his end. However, James Dean's fatal crash was on the way to a race meeting, not racing against the clock. The 550 Spyder had success not only in the United States, but also in Europe and even in the Carrera Panamericana race. This Mexican street race was the toughest event of its time. Porsche entered a car developing only 117 hp in 1954, facing competitors with much more horsepower. Stuttgart's Hans Herrmann drove the 1,213-lbs (550-kg) lightweight racing car to third place, holding numerous much more powerful cars at bay. It was the classic David versus Goliath line-up. 1956 saw the car storm to victory in the Targa Florio with a 15-minute lead.

1954	1.498 CC	117 HP	140 MPH

PORSCHE 911 RS 2.7

"DUCKTAIL"

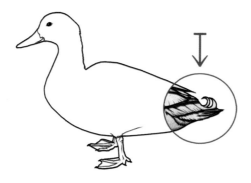

Less is more. Porsche has successfully lived by this philosophy for some time. Paring down to add value: Reduced weight, less equipment, higher performance, more fun—and of course more money. This less-is-more plaything guarantees customers more prestige and faster lap times, making the RS models a superb basis for racing. The 911 Carrera RS 2.7 created a real big bang in 1972. Its striking rear spoiler was designed to increase downforce on the drive axle and gave rise to its popular nickname "Ducktail." The resemblance to a harmless water bird is a curious story, because the RS was the sharpest shot of its day. The six-cylinder engine, bored out to 2.7 liters, developed 210 hp—four times the power of the boxer engine of the VW Beetle. The performance of the 911 RS matches that of immeasurably more powerful Ferraris costing almost twice the 36,500 German Mark price tag of the Porsche. The unbeatable combination of lightweight construction and outstanding engine performance that made the Porsche so famous in the 1960s still burns brightly today. Over the decades, the RS has developed into the GT3 model range, causing a stir on both road and race track.

1972-1973	2.687 CC	210 HP	150 MPH

PORSCHE 917 LH

"HIPPIE CAR"

Used by Martini Racing, although with a different paint scheme to later cars, this is the long-tail 917 that finished in second place at Le Mans in 1970. Its unique paint job meant it soon trended as the "Hippie Car." The psychedelic colors with swooping green and white stripes on a purple background were a good reason for that. Anatole Lapine, the Stuttgart car manufacturer's newly appointed design chief, was the man behind this look. Some insiders claim that more than 1,500 spray cans were used to paint the car. Driven by the Franco-German duo of Gérard Larrousse and Willi Kauhsen, the number 3 car completed Porsche's historic double victory. The Hippie 917 generally had the best opportunities, ensuring it was a frontrunner towards the end of the 24-hour race. The long tail meant that higher speeds of up to 210 mph (340 km/h) were possible. However, the chaotic race with ever-changing weather conditions and numerous tire stops, including the favorite Ferraris, frequently shuffled the classification order. At the end of the race, Larrousse and Kauhsen and their "Hippie Car" finished five laps down.

1970	4.494 CC	520 HP	210 MPH

PORSCHE 917/30

"CANAM KILLER"

0 to 60 mph (100 km/h) in 2.1 seconds, reaching 125 mph (200 km/h) in 5.3 seconds and up to 185 mph (300 km/h) in 11.3 seconds. Performance like this sounds almost too good to be true, but the Porsche 917/30 made it a reality. The 1973 launch model was the most powerful version of the successful 917 sports car. After a change of rules, Porsche was no longer able to enter the 917 in the 1972 World Sportscar Championship. Ferdinand Piëch was on the hunt for another playing field with the CanAm series in Canada and the US in his sights. Initially, turbo technology was completely unknown territory. Chief engineer Hans Mezger nevertheless managed to tame the undriveable beast. After the 917/10 variant won the race series in 1972, the 917/30 matched this victory a year later. By the end of its development, the 5.4-liter twin turbo V12 produced 1,100 hp. The American V8 fireballs, with a maximum permitted capacity of up to 8 liters, were kept firmly in check. Mark Donohue could win at will in 1973, in the car he named the "CanAm Killer." With a top speed of 255 mph (414 km/h), the 917/30 was the fastest car ever to race. The CanAm series was suspended due to the 1974 oil crisis, so the 917/16, originally planned to have a 16-cylinder engine, never took to the track for a single race.

1973-1975	5.374 CC	1.100 HP	235-255 MPH

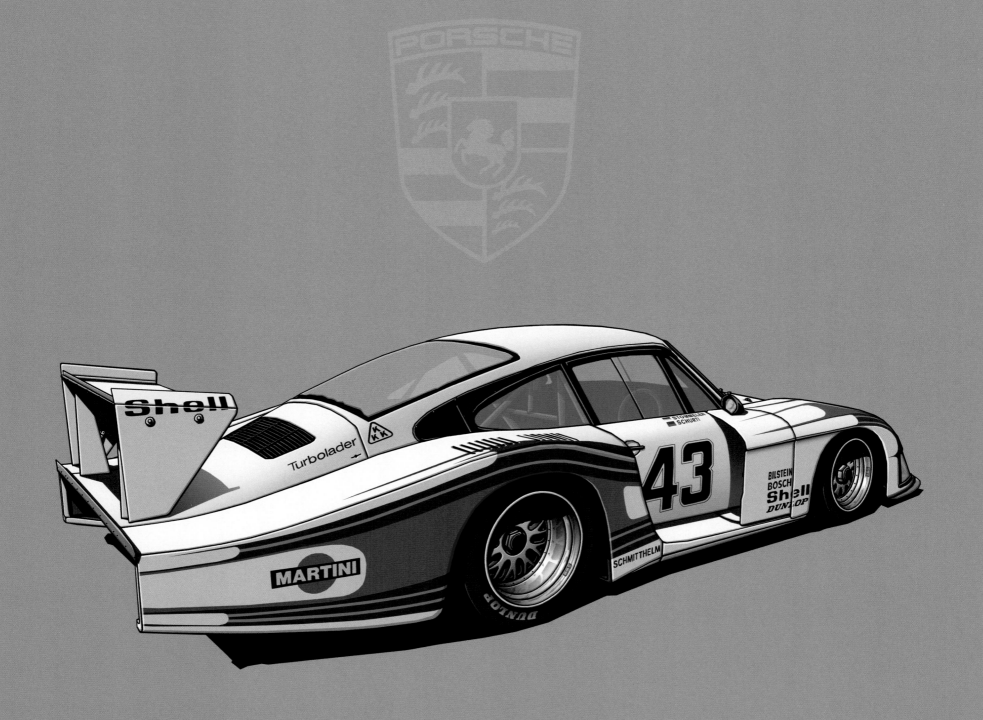

PORSCHE 935

"YELLOW TEAPOT"

Rarely has a name been so closely paired with the Renault turbo experiment as that of Jean-Pierre Jabouille. In 1979, the Frenchman landed the first ever win for a turbocharged Formula 1 car. Yet, two years elapsed before he could capitalize on this. Renault experts predicted it would be a potential winner thanks to the example set by Porsche. The Stuttgart team had established turbo technology in sports car design. Renault launched the RS01 in 1977. A small V6 at only 1.5 liters, it still gave an output of 500 hp, making the turbo engine just as powerful as, e.g., the V12 engine in Nikki Lauda's Ferrari 312 T2. The French were hampered by reliability glitches with their engine: the V6 turbo frequently made a spectacle of itself with engine explosions. White smoke would billow from the car, so British spectators would cruelly joke around, dubbing the Renault RS01 the "Yellow Teapot." As nicknames go, that's fair: a yellow kettle would emit clouds of white smoke when on the boil. It took until 1979, before the silliness stopped. Jean-Pierre Jabouille won his home race in Dijon with the much improved RS10, which had replaced the RS01 over the course of the season. Even with super-star Alain Prost on board, Renault never managed to bring the Formula 1 title home to France, finishing second again in 1983 in both the drivers' and constructors' standings.

1977-1979	1.492 CC	500 HP	N/A

ROLLS-ROYCE SILVER CLOUD III

"CHINESE EYES"

You gotta hand it to the experts at Rolls-Royce. They pick a great model name: Silver Cloud, Ghost, Phantom, Corniche, or Silver Seraph. These British luxury cars all have dignified, august labels, cultivating an aura of mystique. Other manufacturers were welcome to try out cryptic number configurations, or to hire agencies that churn out names with the 'wow' effect. The Great British public would likely frown at this commercialism. Rolls-Royce bosses must have been taken aback when the public scathingly dubbed one of their models "Chinese Eye." That's what happened to the Rolls-Royce Silver Cloud III, a two-door limousine produced between 1962 and 1965, and available as a convertible coupé or roadster. Yet a Norwegian designer created the Rolls design with the "Chinese Eyes." By the time his design ventured onto the road, he had left for the fjords. The Silver Cloud has the classic car caché—at least one celebrity is a registered owner. Supermodel Kate Moss chose the Rolls with the controversial front end back in 2007.

1962-1965	6.230 CC	N/A	110 MPH

ROVER P5

„POOR MAN'S ROLLS-ROYCE"

The Brits love to classify things as a "Poor Man's...". They always have a pigeonhole waiting for a car. The Rover P5 was reminiscent of a smaller version of the luxury cars from Crewe. An imposing chrome grille, distinguished bodywork design lines, and a classy interior give appropriately under-stated appeal. The P5 was not only popular with wealthy bankers in London's financial metropolis; members of the government were also seen in demurely painted Rovers. Even Her Majesty Queen Elizabeth was a lover of the four-door sedan. Dated straight-six engines were used until 1967, when they were replaced by a V8 bought in from Buick, and subsequently modified. The Rover P5 now had essentially the same engine as a Rolls-Royce under the hood. Unlike their bigger role model, Rover obligingly published exact horsepower figures and didn't bluster with vague terms like "enough." One detail of the Rover P5 coupé version is noteworthy: it created a new vehicle class—the four-door coupé. Unlike an ordinary, four-door sedan, the car had a lowered roof and smaller windows to reveal a pleasing new design. Much later, the British were regarded as trendsetters, bringing other manufac-turers onto the same page: Mercedes was the first to copy the concept with the CLS, but Audi, BMW, Maserati, and VW soon followed.

1958-1973	2.995-3.528 CC	117-158 HP	100-120 MPH

SHELBY TURBINE INDY CAR

"JET RACER"

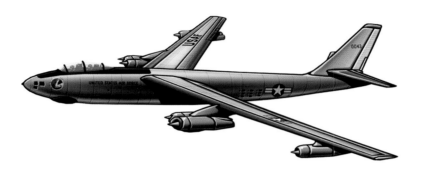

The Shelby Turbine Indy Car has pride of place in the list of "racing car wannabes." Racing driver and constructor Carroll Shelby watched the near-win of the STP-Paxton Turbocar in 1967. It was only three laps short of the first major win for a turbine car in the Indy 500, the most famous race on the US calendar. Motivated by that race, Shelby wanted to make the big win possible in the next year's race. A General Electric turbo would provide the necessary power, with F1 professionals Bruce McLaren and Denny Hulme planned to take the wheel of the two cars. However, his ambitious plans suffered a cruel setback when the rules were changed to limit air intake for turbine cars, so Shelby's "Jet Racer" had to put up with reduced top speed—a fatal move in oval racing at that time when average speeds commonly exceeded 150 mph (240 km/h). Developer Ken Wallace tried to outsmart the event organizers: he cheated with the air intake to keep the loss of power as minimal as possible. However, the deception came out, chief designer Phil Remington left the team and the Shelby Turbine "Jet Racer" was never raced.

1968	N/A	N/A	N/A

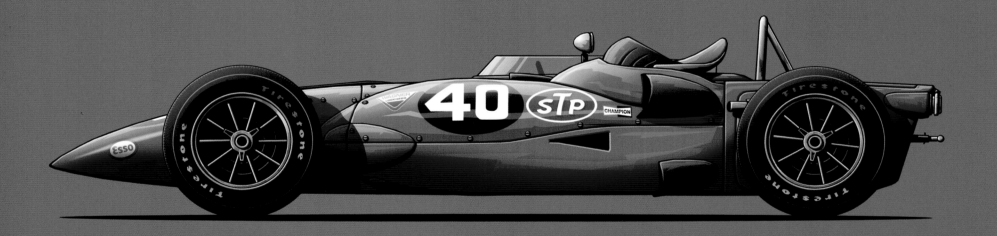

STP-PAXTON TURBOCAR

"SILENT SAM"

[▬ ▬ ▬]

Self-driving cars that are lookalike UFOs? Or one better: Flying cars that travel at the speed of light. Anything was possible in Americans' wildest dreams. Spurred on by early 1960s' optimism for progress, aircraft turbines were also fitted to cars. The logic was that it would only be a matter of time before they ousted the piston engine. To give the idea wings, the STP-Paxton Turbocar lined up on the grid for the famous Indy 500 in 1967. The project's budget was underwritten by mineral oil company STP, an active motorsport sponsor back in the day. The Pratt & Whitney turbine mounted alongside the driver produced 550 hp and its power was directed to all four wheels—another innovation. Its driver, Parnelli Jones, almost caused a sensation at the legendary Indy 500. It seemed like victory was a sure thing for the red racing car, until three laps before the checkered flag, a small transmission part failed. It was the end of the dream. A. J. Foyt in the Coyote-Ford landed the win. The STP-Paxton Turbocar was known as "Silent Sam," because the turbine car sounded completely different to conventional cars with their roaring V8 engines.

1967	N/A	550 HP	N/A

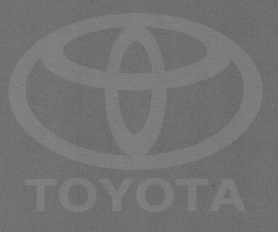

TOYOTA LAND CRUISER FJ55

"IRON PIG"

Tough, robust, and unpretentious, the Toyota Land Cruiser was the go-to vehicle for excursions over rough terrain. Created as the J4 in 1965, the second generation FJ55 (launched in 1967) proved its ability on any dirt road, savannah, or desert trail. "Iron Pig" is a play on its character as an automotive workhorse. Even when used and abused, the Japanese Jeep-like vehicle proved virtually indestructible. Of course, its solid construction was the foundation, albeit with an effect on its weight. It was no surprise that the public was enthusiastic about assigning similar common animal names to other vehicles—for instance, armored personnel carriers or especially big motorcycles. The design suited the "Iron Pig" label; it was not one for wimps. Form conspicuously followed function—you notice this on all the corners and edges. As with all the Land Cruisers, the FJ55 was made for a lengthy period. Four-door production continued from 1967 to 1980. This gnarly off-roader garnered power exclusively from straight six-cylinder engines. The 3.8 to 4.2-liter gas engines produced between 122 and 135 hp.

1967-1980	3.778-4.230 CC	122-135 HP	75-100 MPH

TRABANT 601

"RACING CARDBOARD"

Germany has at least a handful of famous cars. The "Käfer/Beetle," "Flügeltürer/Gullwing," "Barockengel/Baroque Angel," or "Badewanne/Bathtub," were joined by the renowned "Rennpappe/Racing Cardboard." From 1958, many East German citizens got around using the Trabant. The 601 was launched in 1964, and was built in bulk numbers until 1990. Over its long-lasting construction in Zwickau, Saxony, the Trabant spelled shortage, the failure of the planned economy, and technical stagnation. The car barely changed over its lifetime. As time passed, it grew estranged from modern technical standards. The East German government stubbornly blocked any progress. After the autumn of 1989, the Trabant 601 became a global symbol for the fall of the Berlin Wall, the end of the Iron Curtain, and the reunification of Germany. With a top speed of 70 mph (110 km/h), the Trabant had a reputation as a lame duck, although its two-stroke engine always sounded rather like a souped up moped. So much for the first part of its nickname. The second part is down to the construction of the diminutive car: the bodywork was not made completely of sheet steel, like modern cars. The outer skin was made of Duroplast, a resin impregnated plastic. Strictly speaking, only one Trabant model—P 800 RS—should have suited the "Racing Cardboard" nickname. Its two-stroke engine was tuned to 65 hp for the rally version, giving a top speed of up to 125 mph (165 km/h). In East Germany, the Trabant was also known as the "Walking Frame," "Roofed Sparkplug," or "Plastic Bomber."

1964-1990	594 CC	26 HP	70 MPH

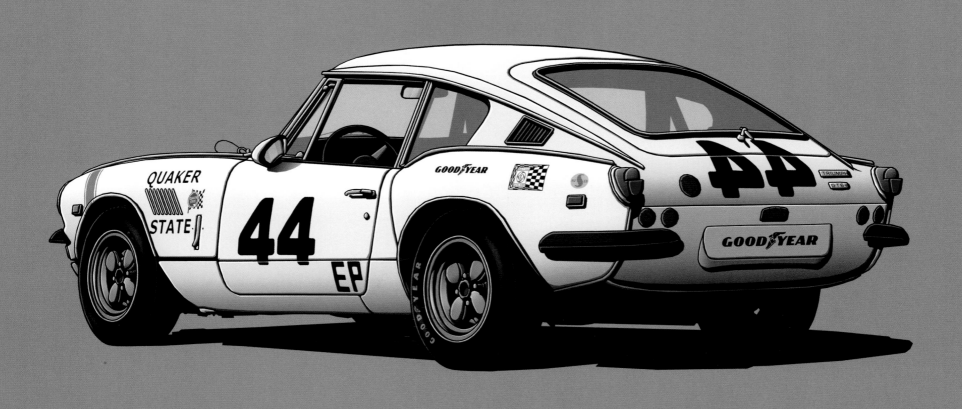

TRIUMPH GT6

"POOR MAN'S E-TYPE"

Triumph gained a reputation for commissioning foreign designers to craft its cars: Italy's Michelotti was responsible for the design blueprints of the TR4, and German company Karmann took on its successor, the TR6. They also lined up other projects for Michelotti: his skills were called on for the successful Spitfire roadster and its enclosed variant, the Triumph GT6. Unlike the open Spitfire, the GT6 had a straight six-cylinder engine, but without the TR5's 2.5-liter engine it was a modified 2.0-liter version of the Triumph Vitesse. To fit the long engine into such a small car, it was designed with a power bulge in the hood. The fastback rear with the large tailgate was a confusing, Jaguar E-Type look-alike. The small sports car also aped its larger role model from the side. What could be more appropriate than to nickname this Triumph a "Poor Man's E-Type?" Of course, a glance at its price tag revealed the GT6 was in a different league from the Jaguar, and even a poor guy could afford an E-Type... well perhaps, at a stretch. Just like its bigger role model, the Triumph two-seater also regularly participated in the motorsport world.

1966-1973	1.998 CC	95-104 HP	100-105 MPH

TYRRELL P34

"SIX-WHEELER"

Cars with six wheels? Not exactly a trailblazing success. Mind you, it wasn't necessarily a bad idea: four small front wheels were intended to reduce air resistance as well as to improve traction in fast cornering. The "Six-Wheeler" was officially known as the P34 and was unveiled at the 1976 Spanish Grand Prix. Its radical design from chief designer Derek Gardner was regarded with awe in the paddock. Yet, it wasn't until the season's second race that industry experts would know if the concept had high potential. The P34 retired in Spain, but Jody Scheckter finished fourth at the race in Belgium. The South African driver also stood on the podium at the Swedish Grand Prix. The Tyrrell didn't log any further wins, primarily due to its special front tires: Goodyear couldn't—and didn't care to—develop further. Scheckter quit the team at the end of 1976, and remarked that the "Six-Wheeler" was "a piece of junk." Patrick Depailler and Ronnie Peterson drove for Tyrrell in 1977, but neither driver scored a win. F1 rules were changed to ban six-wheeled cars, so other cars like those from Ferrari, March, or Williams with four driven wheels never made it onto the grid. However, the veteran Tyrrell "Six-Wheeler" has survived, and can still be seen today at historic racing events.

1976	2.993 CC	425 HP	N/A

VAUXHALL FIRENZA

"BABY BERTHA"

The world oil crisis was a rough time for sports cars. British carmaker Vauxhall realized it and had to make some design adjustments. In 1973, the Firenza was given a new front end to freshen up the coupé's conservative appearance. And to tempt buyers, the 2.3-liter four-cylinder engine was simultaneously tuned to produce 132 hp. HP, short for High Performance, was the official suffix for this two-door coupé, although it was commonly known as the "Droopsnoot" due to its overhanging nose. A special racing Firenza highlighted the sporty image of the Firenza HP. The basic quality destined to mesmerize the fans was its 500 hp, fire-spitting V8 engine, with an utterly unforgettable, brutal racing sound. The Firenza secured 40 wins out of 43 races. Gary Marshall, a burly six-and-a-half footer (2 m tall), was behind the wheel for wild battles with the pack of Ford Escort, Capri, and Skoda 130 RS racing cars. His sweeping successes on mostly British circuits led to the Firenza being dubbed "Baby Bertha," after a rocket with a similarly resounding effect. Despite their best efforts, and some impressive wins, Vauxhall only sold 200 Firenzas. The aggressive "Droopsnoot" front end with dual headlamps mounted behind glass still lived on. It was also copied by Ford for the Escort RS 2000 Mk II and the Sierra.

1974	4.949 CC	500 HP	N/A

VOLVO P1800 ES

"SNOW WHITE'S COFFIN"

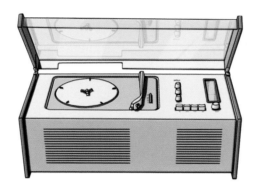

Who would have predicted it? The Volvo P 1800 ES, with its alternative rear end, would be considered a template for modern fast station wagons. When the two-door version came to market in 1971, the design hardly earned a popular reaction from the motoring masses. The all-glass rear, with a frameless rear windshield challenged run-of-the-mill expectations. Volvo's managers were trying to revive the normal P 1800 sedan. The ordinary coupé had been on the market since 1961, selling particularly well in the US. It was famous for its role as the company car driven by Simon Templar, played by Roger Moore, in the TV series *The Saint*. The slightly outlandish appearance of the new all-glass variant prompted comparisons with Snow White's glass coffin—the heroine was poisoned by the Queen in Grimm's fairy tale and then lay in state in a similar coffin. From that point on, Volvo's coupé was known as "Snow White's Coffin." That said, the classy four-seater was practical—the sports wagon was easy to load through the large glass tailgate. Volvo's later attempt (30 years on) to evoke memories of the legendary P 1800 ES, based on the C 30 compact car, was not a stunning success. A myth cannot be conjured out of marketing spin.

1971-1973	1.986 CC	124 HP	115 MPH

VW BEETLE

"HERBIE"

The Beetle "Herbie" is one of those iconic movie cars whose fame outshines the lead actor's. What's so surprising? "Herbie" was the star character. The Beetle with the magic powers first caused a stir in 1968, when it bewitched audiences in *The Love Bug*. Disney made a fortune from the sequels *Herbie Rides Again* (1974,) *Herbie Goes to Monte Carlo* (1976,) *Herbie Goes Bananas* (1980,) the five-part TV series *Herbie, The Love Bug* (1982,) and a TV film also entitled *The Love Bug* (1997). The year 2005 saw the release of what is currently the last big screen movie: *Herbie: Fully Loaded* with Lindsay Lohan, Matt Dillon, and Michael Keaton in starring roles. Not forgetting "Herbie", the miracle Beetle bore the number 53. "Herbie" can drive itself. It is lightning fast; it can scale walls and even has anthropomorphic qualities. Most of all, this is a modern fairy-tale classic in which the Beetle—with just 34 hp—helps the unlucky racing driver Jim Douglas win races against the odds of more powerful racing cars like an AC Cobra or Jaguar E-Type. Incidentally, Jim Douglas was played by the actor Dean Jones.

1963	N/A	N/A	N/A

VW KDF-WAGEN

"BEETLE"

The story of the legendary VW "Beetle" is complex, yet intriguing. In 1934, Adolf Hitler commissioned Ferdinand Porsche to design an inexpensive Volkswagen, a car for the people. The official label was the "KdF-Wagen." KdF was short for "Strength Through Joy" ("Kraft durch Freude"). This was a state-controlled organization in Nazi Germany tasked to promote leisure activities, surveillance, and to establish a system of "coordination" or "Gleichschaltung." The early prototypes based on the NSU and Zündapp models were not pursued, so the world-famous "Beetle" was born in 1938. *The New York Times* even acknowledged the little German car and that same year published an article, which first referred to the "Beetle." Delayed by the war, series production only began in 1946, with exports to the US following in 1950. The "Beetle" nickname, inspired by its rounded bodywork, quickly became popular here. The common name in Germany remained the Volkswagen. It was only upon the release of the VW 1500 Type 3 that the term "Beetle" entered everyday usage to differentiate it from its big brother. The world-famous model from Wolfsburg was also known as the "Kugelporsche," or "Round Porsche." Sales of the "Beetle" totaled 21.5 million vehicles during the period 1938 to 2003. The "Beetle" was manufactured in 20 other countries besides Germany. The last place to halt production of the Volkswagen "Beetle" was Mexico.

1938-1939	985 CC	22 HP	60 MPH

VW T1

"BUS"

What an incredible career the VW "Bus" enjoyed when compared with other automobiles. Back in 1950, its market launch revealed a pragmatic big bro' to the "Beetle." Rear engine, air cooled, with an output of 25 hp—its look, unique face and large, rounded headlamps, its split front windshield, and striking nose on the front panel make the "Bus" utterly irresistible, now as much as then. It is also blissful nostalgia for the hippie era, when this colorfully painted utility wagon travelled the country as a home and a dream on wheels. This multitalented T1—also known as the "Hippie Van"—has undergone an amazing transformation: from the workhorse and camper wagon of Germany's Economic Miracle days, to the cult hippie bus and everybody's darling. Today, fans of the first VW Bus pay high sums, especially for the sought-after Samba Bus with two-tone paintwork, fabric sunroof, and typically eight extra windows. The unfavorable relationship between supply (extremely low) and demand (extremely high) made this first VW Bus pricey. Unmodified original models are virtually non-existent, because rust prevention to modern standards simply didn't exist in the 1950s. The finest veteran models have all been restored, without exception. This entails painstaking work, particularly for the "Bus." Opinions are divided on the origin of the car's nickname in Germany: "Bulli." Some suggest a combination of "bus" ("Bus") and "delivery wagon" ("Lieferwagen"), while others highlight the original German *bullig*, meaning "beefy." That was the key word VW workers used during the vehicle's development.

1950-1967	1.131-1.493 CC	25-44 HP	55-70 MPH

WILLYS MB

"JEEP"

Jeep fans can sing the praises of a US Military call for bids that spawned production of this special off-road vehicle. Better still, this established a brand. Without the Willys MB, designed to rise to the challenges of the Second World War, we would now be without Cherokees or Renegades. In 1940, the US Army needed an all-terrain vehicle that could be produced cheaply and in large quantities. Willys Overland, Bantam, and Ford set to work. Willys got the order, while Ford also produced vehicles under license. The result was known as the Willys MB or Ford GPW. It could go anywhere and could even be dropped from an aircraft by parachute. For a long while, "Jeep" was a name supposedly derived from the abbreviation "GP," or "General Purpose." Now, some regard that as a red herring. "GP" never crops up on official records. Apparently, "Jeep" may have originated from the comic series "Popeye:" The magical creature "Eugene the Jeep" and his supernatural abilities were always prepared, even when muscleman Popeye got stuck. Parallels with the versatile "Jeep" were apparent. GIs could hardly have suspected that the military vehicle would have an international career ahead of it: the 370,000 veteran Willys "Jeeps" were succeeded by countless post-war successor models. The current Wrangler and its stablemates are basically the great-great-great-great-grand-children of the first "Jeep." In common parlance, the name "Jeep" has long come to be a generic term, much like "kleenex" or "xerox."

1942-1945	2.199 CC	60 HP	65 MPH

INDEX / Cars

Helge Jepsen's career as an illustrator began at age eight: from 1974 to 1979, he garnered (non-monetary) prizes from drawing contests in the North Frisian town of Bredstedt. Later, *Stern, Der Spiegel, Men's Health, Playboy, Wirtschaftswoche, ramp* and many other magazines talent-spotted the qualified communications design specialist, who was also acquainted with most of the top advertising agencies. Helge Jepsen has lived and worked in Essen since his graduation. When not engrossed in illustration, he is an avid world traveler or enjoys driving his British classic—naturally, a nicknamed car.

Michael Köckritz first had the ambition of becoming a doctor, yet soon after graduating in medicine he discovered his passion for journalism and advertising. Initially, he worked as a freelance photographer and writer before becoming co-editor of the lifestyle car magazine *AUTOFOCUS*. In 2007, media specialist Köckritz and partners launched the independent publishing company RED INDIANS—an innovative "think-and-do-tank" and a lively, creative experimental platform for strategic content marketing. As publisher and editor-in-chief, he develops trendsetting magazine formats with titles like *ramp, CAPZ, rampstyle, rampdesign* and, recently, *Weiberkram* that have won multiple national and international awards.

© 2017 teNeues Media GmbH & Co. KG, Kempen
Illustrations © 2017 Helge Jepsen
All rights reserved

Illustrations/Design/Layout: Helge Jepsen, www.helgejepsen.de
Editorship/Texts: Michael Köckritz
Editing: Matthias Mederer, Frank Mühling and the editorial team of Red Indians/ramp
Copy editing (German version): Korrekturbüro Burger, www.korrekturburger.de
Translation (British English)/coordination: Wendy Rees/Dr Suzanne Kirkbright
Copy editing (American English): Reid Parkinson
Production by Dieter Haberzettl, teNeues Media
Editorial coordination: Pit Pauen, Inga Wortmann, teNeues Media

Published by teNeues Publishing Group

teNeues Media GmbH & Co. KG
Am Selder 37, 47906 Kempen, Germany
Phone: +49-(0)2152-916-0
Fax: +49-(0)2152-916-111
e-mail: books@teneues.com

Press department: Andrea Rehn
Phone: +49-(0)2152-916-202
e-mail: arehn@teneues.com

teNeues Publishing Company
7 West 18th Street, New York, NY 10011, USA
Phone: +1-212-627-9090
Fax: +1-212-627-9511

teNeues Publishing UK Ltd.
12 Ferndene Road, London SE24 0AQ, UK
Phone: +44-(0)20-3542-8997

teNeues France S.A.R.L.
39, rue des Billets, 18250 Henrichemont, France
Phone: +33-(0)2-4826-9348
Fax: +33-(0)1-7072-3482

www.teneues.com

ISBN 978-3-8327-6927-7

Library of Congress Number: 2016963278

Printed in Italy

The Deutsche Nationalbibliothek lists this publication in the Deutsche Nationalbibliografie; detailed bibliographic data are available on the Internet at http://dnb.dnb.de.

teNeues Publishing Group
Kempen
Berlin
London
Munich
New York
Paris

teNeues